Essentials of a Qualitative Doctorate

Qualitative Essentials

Series Editor: Janice Morse
University of Utah

Series Editorial Board: H. Russell Bernard, Kathy Charmaz, D. Jean Clandinin, Juliet Corbin, Carmen de la Cuesta, John Engel, Sue E. Estroff, Jane Gilgun, Jeffrey C. Johnson, Carl Mitcham, Katja Mruck, Judith Preissle, Jean J. Schensul, Sally Thorne, John van Maanen, Max van Manen

Qualitative Essentials is a book series providing a comprehensive but succinct overview of topics in qualitative inquiry. These books will fill an important niche in qualitative methods for students—and others new to the qualitative research— who require rapid but complete perspective on specific methods, strategies, and important topics. Written by leaders in qualitative inquiry, alone or in combination, these books will be an excellent resource for instructors and students from all disciplines. Proposals for the series should be sent to the series editor at explore@lcoastpress.com.

Titles in this series:

Naturalistic Observation, Michael V. Angrosino

Essentials of Qualitative Inquiry, Maria J. Mayan

Essentials of Field Relationships, Amy Kaler and Melanie A. Beres

Essentials of Accessible Grounded Theory, Phyllis Norerager Stern and Caroline Jane Porr

Essentials of Qualitative Interviewing, Karin Olson

Essentials of Transdisciplinary Research, Patricia Leavy

Essentials of a Qualitative Doctorate, Immy Holloway and Lorraine Brown

Focus Group Research, Martha Ann Carey and Jo-Ellen Asbury

Essentials of a Qualitative Doctorate

Immy Holloway

Lorraine Brown

Left Coast Press Inc.

Walnut Creek, California

green press INITIATIVE

Left Coast Press, Inc. is committed to preserving ancient forests and natural resources. We elected to print this title on 30% post consumer recycled paper processed chlorine free. As a result, for this printing, we have saved:

1 Tree (40' tall and 6-8" diameter)
1 Million BTUs of Total Energy
114 Pounds of Greenhouse Gases
620 Gallons of Wastewater
42 Pounds of Solid Waste

Left Coast Press, Inc. made this paper choice because our printer, Thomson-Shore, Inc., is a member of Green Press Initiative, a nonprofit program dedicated to supporting authors, publishers, and suppliers in their efforts to reduce their use of fiber obtained from endangered forests.

For more information, visit www.greenpressinitiative.org

Environmental impact estimates were made using the Environmental Defense Paper Calculator. For more information visit: www.papercalculator.org.

LEFT COAST PRESS, INC.
1630 North Main Street, #400
Walnut Creek, CA 94596
www.LCoastPress.com

ISBN 978-1-61132-138-8 hardback
ISBN 978-1-61132-139-5 paperback
ISBN 978-1-61132-676-5 consumer eBook

Library of Congress Cataloging-in-Publication Data:

Holloway, Immy.
    Essentials of a qualitative doctorate / Immy Holloway, Lorraine Brown.
    p. cm. — (Qualitative essentials)
    Includes bibliographical references.
    ISBN 978-1-61132-138-8 (hardback) — ISBN 978-1-61132-139-5 (paperback) — ISBN 978-1-61132-676-5 (consumer eBook)
    1. Dissertations, Academic—Handbooks, manuals, etc. 2. Qualitative research—Handbooks, manuals, etc. I. Brown, Lorraine, 1961-II. Title.
    LB2369.H65 2012
    8.02—dc23
                        2012022874

Printed in the United States of America

∞™ The paper used in this publication meets the minimum requirements of American National Standard for Information Sciences—Permanence of Paper for Printed Library Materials, ANSI/NISO Z39.48–1992.

Contents

THE RESEARCH JOURNEY

THE FINAL STAGE

Acknowledgments

We would like to thank the series editor Professor Janice Morse for her advice and support. Thanks are also due to our publisher Mitch Allen and his staff, and in particular to our copy editor, Stacey Cobbett Sawyer. We are grateful to our colleagues Dr. Karen Rees and Dr. Jan Walker, as well as to the doctorate students who helped us with our questions and from whom we learned so much.

Immy Holloway and Lorraine Brown
August 2012

Introduction: The Qualitative Doctorate

This book is intended for doctoral candidates who write their dissertations in English, and in English-speaking countries. We are well aware that the doctoral process and some aspects of the language associated with doctoral study differ across such countries, although the major elements of the doctoral journey and terminology are similar. Many places, for example, the United States and Canada, require students to complete work in addition to the doctoral dissertation. In Britain, doctoral students are asked to attend research and ethics sessions in addition to writing a thesis, but these training sessions are not usually assessed. Professional doctorates always include an element of work relating to practice and are more vocationally orientated, but the standards of doctorates are similar in many English-speaking and Nordic countries. There is also a doctorate by publication, which is discussed in Chapter 10. We do not use the term *Ph.D.* in this text, because other forms of the doctorate exist, and this book aims to be useful also to students who undertake other types of doctoral studies.

You might ask: What can I do with a doctorate? Is it worth the effort? What can I achieve? The Research Councils in the United Kingdom (RCUK, 2010) in collaboration with the Careers Research and Advisory Centre (CRAC) have examined some of the destinations of doctorate students in the United Kingdom and the value a doctorate holds for employers. A high percentage (44 percent) go into higher education research or

Essentials of a Qualitative Doctorate by Immy Holloway and Lorraine Brown, 11–14

lecturing occupations; others go into specialist roles in health and social work; yet others work in research and development or manufacturing. The figures for the European Union are similar, although they differ slightly. If you have a doctorate it is more likely that you will gain a good salary and higher work satisfaction. Both of us completed a doctorate mainly for our own satisfaction, although it has helped our careers, particularly through publishing papers, books, and doing further research. We learned a great deal in our respective areas, and we are still motivated to learn more. Occasionally the doctoral journey was hard, and we had some of the same problems that you will face during the process of doing your doctorate.

Dozens of books exist that give detailed advice, and some of them are very helpful. Our book includes only essentials for the qualitative doctorate specifically. Although this book may sometimes sound too prescriptive, it is not meant to be. You always have the freedom to do what you wish within the limits of your institutional guidelines. We present only suggestions to make the doctoral journey easier for you, not rigid rules.

In making these suggestions, we've tried to incorporate the most important aspects of the qualitative doctorate. We would advise you to read all the chapters before you start, but read and reread Chapters 8, 9, and 10 in particular, because these cover the main processes as well as the traps and problems of doctoral work.

Differences between Countries

We need to clarify some terms and practices before you read this book. In the United States, the completed doctoral script is called a *dissertation*; in the United Kingdom, it is referred to as a *thesis*; the term *dissertation* indicates a master's study in the United Kingdom. Canada, Australia, and many other countries follow the British model. The requirements are also somewhat different for a number of countries; some doctorates demand a large input of theory, others do not. In the United Kingdom, the transfer or upgrade to the doctorate is an important stage of the journey.

> *All doctoral students need to be sure of the requirements in their country and their institution.*

All universities examine the doctorate, but not all do so orally. In the United States the oral defense is conducted by a dissertation committee and is known as the doctoral defense; in the United Kingdom it is conducted by an examination panel, and it is called *viva voce* (usually referred to in short as *viva*). Australia's universities do not require an oral defense. Whereas in U.S. universities students have a committee that advises and examines, and an advisor who is the main contact with the student throughout,

This photo shows how the Department of Caring Science, Åbo Akademi, Vasa, Finland, announces the completion of the doctoral dissertation. The tradition of hammering the dissertation to a tree comes from the action of Martin Luther, who nailed his theses to a church door.

U.K. and Australian students interact with one or, more usually now, two supervisors, who meet students regularly and often. They offer guidance throughout the research process.

In this book, for the sake of consistency and to avoid repetition, the North American terms *advisor, dissertation,* and *oral defense* will be used instead of the U.K. terms *supervisor, thesis,* and *viva.*

1. Perspectives on Qualitative Research

You have decided to do a qualitative doctorate. Why did you make this decision? Did you find that your research question demanded a qualitative approach? Did you prefer the qualitative approach to quantitative inquiry? Do you think that qualitative research is easier?

We discuss the last question first, because many researchers carry out qualitative inquiry believing that it is easy to do. If this is your reason, you will not be able to justify your research—but such justification is an important part of the rationale that you set out in your introduction and methodology chapters. In any case, a good piece of qualitative research is just as demanding as a quantitative study, although for different reasons, which will become clearer during the course of your dissertation.

Qualitative research will give you insight into various perspectives on a phenomenon, on behaviors and feelings, and it allows a deep exploration of different experiences. Researchers study people in their natural surroundings and build up relationships so they can learn to see the world from the participants' point of view, on the basis of a common humanity and sometimes a shared culture, although they can never put themselves wholly into "other people's shoes." Richards and Morse (2007) give you an overview of the type of questions that require a qualitative approach—for instance, seeking knowledge in an area where little is known, where you wish to explore participants' understanding in depth, when you are generating a theory or theoretical ideas.

Essentials of a Qualitative Doctorate by Immy Holloway and Lorraine Brown, 15–23
© 2012 Left Coast Press, Inc. All rights reserved.

Distinctions between Qualitative and Quantitative Perspectives

The dichotomy between qualitative and quantitative inquiry has been over-simplified, and the "paradigm wars" are ostensibly over. However, you will find that the debate still continues in academic settings—to the frustration of qualitative researchers. There is no room here to discuss these arguments. We instead focus on the nature of qualitative research, which has its base in the human sciences, such as anthropology, sociology, and psychology; indeed, it has its deeper roots in philosophy and history (see Willis, 2007). This methodology explores how people make sense of their perceived reality. Thus this approach cannot ever be completely precise, because human beings do not always act or think logically and in predictable ways.

Qualitative research differs from quantitative inquiry in

- its perspectives on the nature of being and reality;
- the type of knowledge that is being sought;
- the amount of knowledge that already exists in the area of study;
- the way the research question is approached;
- the collection and analysis of data;
- the presentation of findings.

These issues connect with the concepts of ontology, epistemology, and methodology. Researchers' assumptions on how the social world can best be studied determine the way the research is shaped. Ontology concerns the nature of existence and reality. Epistemology refers to the theory of knowledge and deals with questions such as what counts as valid knowledge (see also Willis, 2007, p. 10). On these ideas researchers base their methodology—the principles in which their research methods and procedures are rooted. (Ontological, epistemological, and methodological issues are also discussed in Creswell [2007].) Table 1.1 summarizes some of the differences between qualitative and quantitative approaches.

Essential Features of Qualitative Research

Chapter 10 includes a summary of the major traits of qualitative research that you need to take into account throughout your study, including the structure of the dissertation. You probably have already looked through several books on qualitative research, and maybe you have a Master's that

Table 1.1 Some differences between qualitative and quantitative social research (These differences are not absolute, nor are they exhaustive; they are mainly at the end of a continuum between qualitative and quantitative research.) Source: Holloway and Wheeler (2010)

	Qualitative	Quantitative
Aim	Exploration, understanding, and description of participants' experiences and life world Generation of theory from data	Search for causal explanations Testing hypothesis, prediction, control
Approach	Initially broadly focused Process oriented Context-bound, mostly natural settings Getting close to the data	Narrow focus Product-oriented Context free, often in laboratory settings
Sampling	Participants, informants Sampling units such as place, time, concepts Purposive and theoretical sampling Flexible sampling that can develop during the research	Respondents, participants (the term *subjects* is now discouraged in the social sciences) Randomized sampling Sample frame fixed before the research starts
Data collection	In-depth nonstandardized interviews Participant observation/fieldwork Documents, diaries, photographs, videos	Questionnaire, standardized interviews Tightly structured observation Documents
Analysis	Thematic or constant comparative analysis, latent content analysis; ethnographic, narrative analysis, etc.	Statistical analysis
Outcome relationships	A story, ethnography, a theory Direct involvement of researcher Research relationship close	Measurable and testable results Limited involvement of researcher with participant
Rigor	Trustworthiness, authenticity Typicality and transferability Validity	Researcher relationship distant Internal/external validity, reliability Generalizability

involved learning about qualitative research. At the end of this book you will find some references that can help you to continue to learn more about qualitative inquiry. In general, Richards and Morse (2007) advise that working, thinking, and reading qualitatively is crucial in qualitative research. Here, however, we discuss the *essential* characteristics of qualitative research.

Most qualitative research approaches share some traits at a similar level of importance:

1. primacy of data: inductive reasoning;
2. contextualization;
3. insider's perspective;
4. thick description;
5. need for a storyline;
6. critical subjectivity;
7. reflexivity.

Primacy of Data: Inductive Reasoning

Qualitative research is—in its initial stages at least—inductive. *Induction* means that inquiry starts with empirical data that have priority for the researcher. Inductive reasoning proceeds from single examples, cases, or instances to more general principles, from specific observation to general ideas; researchers collect data without undue influence from preexisting theories. Thus true qualitative inquiry does not begin with a hypothesis— although it can develop theories or hypotheses from the data. Of course, researchers have their own particular knowledge bases and cannot simply set them aside (see the section on reflexivity toward the end of this chapter). Researchers' *data*, however, have priority, and the study-related statements that researchers make are always grounded in the data; but researchers also employ deductive reasoning, often formulating working propositions and investigating them by collecting additional data. And sometimes researchers use deduction (though some would dispute this) when theoretical ideas and working propositions are developed and then examined.

In this short book, we cannot pursue the debate over inductive versus deductive reasoning in research. The philosopher Windelband (1848– 1915) called the methods starting from individual cases and events *idiographic* (from the Greek *idios*, "private" or "self") and those that seek lawlike generalities *nomothetic* (from the Greek *nomos*, "law"). These terms are still used to describe the differences between qualitative and quantitative methods, but the debate is more complex than can be covered here, as we said. A great number of books can tell you about induction, deduction, and abduction—for example, Mayan (2009), Alvesson and Sköldberg (2009), Schwandt (2007), and other books mentioned at the end of this text.

Contextualization (Contextuality)

All research is context-bound, located in temporal, social, and cultural space. Qualitative inquiry in particular needs *contextualization*, because it focuses on meaning, and meaning emerges through context. Researchers need situated understanding to be able to relate to participants and data, and one of the goals of qualitative research is to grasp a particular context (Willig, 2008). Thus the circumstances and settings in which the data are collected and analyzed become important. All participants, including the researcher, are steeped in their cultural and social context, and this context influences their beliefs and behaviors. The findings, too, are context-specific—hence the difficulty of generalizing from a qualitative study. Schwandt (2007) adds that a context even influences interpretations in that it affects the "form and direction" of interpretation of the researcher and the researched.

To achieve contextualization, researchers need context sensitivity and context intelligence: they should be aware not only of the wider context but also of the specific circumstances and conditions that influence or even determine the research, such as the background of the participants; the locations in which they live, work, and play; and even the physical setting of the inquiry and the researchers' own assumptions. What time does an event occur? What is the setting in which the research takes place? Would the research be different in a different time and place?

You may know Stevie Smith's poem "Not Waving but Drowning,"* which reminds scholars that actions and words might be misinterpreted if the context is not taken into account. Participants' group membership, their gender and/or ethnic background, might affect the research data, findings, and interpretation. Even the relationship between you and the participants will shape the context.

---

* Stevie Smith, "Not Waving but Drowning," from *Collected Poems of Stevie Smith.* Copyright © 1972 [1957] by Stevie Smith. Penguin and New Directions Publishing Corporation.

Context changes meanings: for instance, you might interview a young woman in her own home about her spending habits with her husband and children present. But the questions posed and the answers given might be different in the context of a gym, for example, away from the domestic situation.

Insider's Perspective

The insider's, or *emic*, perspective helps researchers to put themselves in the shoes of the participants and to see the world—at least to some extent—from their point of view. This insider view is necessary for qualitative researchers to gain an understanding of the participants' culture and setting and the sense they make of it. Harris (1976:336) states: "The way to get inside of people's heads is to talk with them, to ask questions about what they think and feel, and this is what the qualitative researcher does."

The term *etic* refers to the outsider's (in this case the researcher's) perspective, that which is observed from outside a group or a subculture. The researcher as analyst reflects on the emic point of view of the participants but also moves back and forth from the emic to the etic in order to take an analytic—and necessarily more abstract and theoretical—view of the data. Both approaches are needed in qualitative inquiry, but this type of inquiry finds its starting point in the emic perspective. Language, too, becomes an element of importance, both local language and the language of the researcher.

The terms *emic* and *etic* (originally coined by the linguistic anthropologist Pike in 1954) have their basis in anthropology, but other social researchers now use them frequently. However, in social science there is no clear agreement about the meanings of these terms; indeed, the original meanings seem to be lost in their present-day use. These concepts are discussed simplistically here: we describe only their overall meanings and their importance to qualitative inquiry and doctoral research.

Thick Description

Contextualization is closely linked to *thick description*. Geertz (1973) borrowed the term from the philosopher Ryle and used it in qualitative anthropological research as a tool for participant observation. Ponterotto (2006), examining its origins and developments, declares that it has now become a qualitative research instrument for many disciplines. Thick description involves detailed and rich description of the actions, behaviors, and words of people, including processes, intentions, and feelings. It involves a portrayal of individuals and groups in their settings and cultural context.

Description needs also to be analytical and theoretical; hence there is rarely description without interpretation.

Denzin (2001), too, discusses the concept of thick description and suggests, as Geertz has, that it does more than record a person's behavior. Behavior and words are influenced by the meaning that experiences have for the participants. The description should carry a feeling of truth for the reader, who is then able to empathize with and relive the experience described. In contrast, *thin description* refers to an account that reports facts only, that lacks detail and is devoid of meanings and intentions. Thin description has its place: for example, early observational notes contain thin description in that they are superficial and factual, but they fail to offer a full portrayal of the setting.

To be able to give a holistic picture, researchers need to spend as much time as possible in the field, to immerse themselves in the participants' world, to have prolonged engagement with it, and to observe closely. It is the description of "being there," as one author writes (Madden, 2010:159), which will make the portrayal faithful to the participants' motivations and intentions as well as to the context. (For a longer discussion read Denzin, 2001.)

Need for a Storyline

The research account in qualitative research is a *narrative,* or story. Sandelowski (1991:161) speaks of "the story in the study, the tale in the theory, the parable in the principle and the drama in the life." A good story rooted in the data helps to produce a good research report. The storyline presents a thick description of the phenomenon under study and the context surrounding it; this narrative thread makes the study coherent. The researchers tell the research story with particular readers in mind whom they address and with whom they interact. If the account is interesting, readers can engage with it. Holloway (2011:970) states that: "Tension and interest in outcomes are essential traits for qualitative inquiry; they make the story readable and its contents communicable, and communication of the findings is, after all, the aim of all research." The account or report of the research, the completed dissertation, should provoke interest and engagement with the text. It is, however, more than a piece of journalism or an imaginative creation and needs a base in evidence.

Subjectivity

Qualitative inquiry often refers to the *subjectivity* of the researcher. Researchers use their subjectivity as a resource, drawing on their own values and background to understand the participants and the meaning these participants give to their experiences, rather than relying on established instruments, which the quantitative researcher often does. The researchers' preexisting knowledge becomes an integral part of the research (see also the next section, Reflexivity). Hence qualitative writers emphasize "intersubjectivity," which refers to a state between subjectivity and objectivity, whereby understanding between participant and researcher is increased owing to shared experiences and values. It may also mean that researchers, because of the interaction between Self and Other, can empathize with the participants as human beings who share the same humanity. Scheff (2007) states that the world of an individual is always partially shared with others; hence subjectivity and intersubjectivity sensitize researchers to the knowledge and conditions they share with participants. Researchers must, however, take a critical stance toward their own assumptions, which means that they identify and examine their own preconceptions before focusing on the shared experience.

The now almost clichéd expression that the *researcher is the research tool* (instrument) means that the study is affected by those who carry out the research, by their background and by the space and time they occupy. Researchers are accountable for their actions; they have responsibility for collecting, analyzing, and interpreting data as well as for interacting and communicating with participants. Therefore, they use the first person when reporting their research—"I did . . . I used . . . in my study . . ."—rather than the third person—"the researcher did . . ." and so on. This kind of expression also means that the writers take responsibility for the research; Geertz (1988) warned decades ago against the "author-evacuated text."

Quantitative researchers are critical of subjectivity as they strive for objectivity, while qualitative writers stress that no research can be totally value-free and objective, especially not qualitative inquiry, which is characterized by personal engagement and immersion in the research setting. Of course, subjectivity and objectivity lie on a continuum. Qualitative inquiry is not wholly subjective, and quantitative inquiry cannot be completely value-neutral or objective. Qualitative researchers do acknowledge and recognize the limitations of subjectivity, even when they use it as a resource. They reflect on their assumptions and preconceptions and make an attempt to "bracket: them; that is, they try not to be unduly influenced by them."

Reflexivity

Subjectivity is directly related to *reflexivity*, which is one of the most important concepts in qualitative research. Willig (2008) differentiates between personal and epistemological reflexivity. *Personal reflexivity* means that researchers' own beliefs, values, and interests affect the inquiry. Researchers must recognize the boundaries of their objectivity, because qualitative research is strongly affected by their identity and assumptions. *Epistemological reflexivity* refers to the research itself and its knowledge base as well as the researchers' involvement with their own experience in the process of the study and the building of the dissertation. This type of reflexivity examines the way the research has been constructed, its design, the problems under investigation, and the assumptions that have been made in its process. Alvesson and Sköldberg (2009) stress that an ongoing process of mutual and continued interaction takes place between the researcher and the phenomenon under study throughout the course of the research. Researchers need not only to recognize but also to acknowledge their own experiences and their influence on the research.

Finlay (2011) advises that researchers engage their own subjectivity through reflexivity. She claims that the researcher is involved in the construction of the research together with the participants, and the results are *co-constituted* (her emphasis, p. 80) between the researcher, the participants, and the context. Finlay distinguishes between reflexivity and reflection—another important concept in qualitative research. *Reflection* means, in her words, "thinking about" something, whereas *reflexivity* means "critical self-awareness," or critical subjectivity. Reflection provides some insight, but reflexivity is a more complex process (which we cannot expand on here; see Finlay, 2011). In summary, reflexivity is a conscious attempt to acknowledge one's own involvement in the inquiry (Holloway, 2008:202).

Reflexivity is a problematic concept: it can deteriorate into "navel gazing" and self-absorption—that is, continuous self-reference. Self-referencing is useful and sometimes necessary for a piece of research to be truly reflexive, but some qualitative researchers are prone to place themselves in the foreground rather than focusing on the other person, the participant. Researchers must practice scholarship rather than indulge in excessive self-reflection and autobiographical disclosures. By facilitating the acknowledgment of the researcher's presence in the study, reflexivity acts to prevent distortion of the data. At its best it enhances the depth as well as the validity of qualitative research (see also Mayan, 2009).

The Initial Stage

2. Selecting a Topic and Finding the Research Question

Most researchers at doctorate level know about the broader area they wish to study, but the selection of a topic and a research question needs careful consideration. Punch (2006) claims that the area of interest, the topic, and the research question are at different levels of abstraction and generality: the area of interest involves a more general consideration; however, the topic and the research question become progressively more specific and focused.

The main questions to ask are these: What is the research all about? What do I want to find out? Initially try to formulate answers in single sentences, such as: My study is about bullying teachers in private schools; my research is about professional decision making in organizations; the study is about critical incidents on hospital wards for elderly people; I want to find out about the link between tourism and cultural change; I'm interested in the influence of brand on purchase decision; my research will be about the motivations of volunteers in sporting events.

Selecting a Topic

The research topic is generally an element in the area of general interest that will have its base in your discipline. You might, for instance, choose it based on

1   your own experience and knowledge;
2. professional, work, or study-related issues that have come to your attention;

Essentials of a Qualitative Doctorate by Immy Holloway and Lorraine Brown, 27–38
© 2012 Left Coast Press, Inc. All rights reserved.

3. the academic literature of your discipline or a conference that you attended;
4. a gap in the literature in your area of interest;
5. research that you suspect is embedded in assumptions or beliefs that are inaccurate to some degree;
6. an interesting issue debated in the media;
7. something in the area of your professors' expertise that they wish you to study;
8. politicians' statements about social or political strategies.

- A health educator found when teaching her subject in a school that adolescents knew the dangers of exposure to too much sun but still exercised no caution. On reflection she decided to study adolescent sun-related behavior.
- In her professional dealings with international students, one researcher found that host contact was problematic. This situation gave her the idea to study students' immersion in a foreign culture.
- A student attended a conference on management research. She listened to a presentation on managers' motivations for selecting their jobs, which led her to the topic of employee motivations. Although this topic might have emerged through extensive study, reading about it would probably not have carried the same weight as experiencing a conference presentation.
- A sports student perceived a gap in the literature about the bullying of athletes by coaches and decided to explore this area.
- A sociology student found that the topic of young people's binge drinking received constant media coverage. When he saw an advertisement for an opportunity to study this at a local university, he applied and studied the nighttime economy and drinking culture of a major beach resort.
- A nursing professor was involved in research into nurse-student mentorship and recruited new researchers to help cover this vast topic. One of the researchers examined a specific area—namely, communication and relationships between students and their mentors.
- Claims in the media by the Chinese government that tourism between Taiwan and China can improve relations between the two countries inspired a student's interest in the topic. A review of the literature showed that this subject is a neglected area.

Choose a topic that is important rather than trivial; otherwise, nobody will be interested in your research, and it will not be significant enough to advance knowledge in your field. Beware, however, of choosing too broad a topic: "social change" would be an important topic but far too large to discuss in a doctoral study, whereas "change in a small publishing business" or "development in a rural hospital" might be more appropriate.

We would advise you not to select a topic that is intimately connected to your personal life, one about which you might have strong feelings and opinions, because you might not be able to suspend your assumptions. (Of course, there are exceptions to this rule if you can approach the research with an open mind, and your experience provides extra motivation to study the topic in depth.) Researchers generally choose a topic that has been under-researched; Stern (1980:20) calls this "investigations in relatively uncharted waters." And, to avoid duplication, determine what topic areas have been covered by other researchers in essential areas in your field.

Some knowledge in the topic area is a prerequisite of developing a dissertation or thesis; the doctoral (Ph.D.) stage is not for learning the principles of a discipline but for acquiring research skills and contributing to knowledge. In addition, interdisciplinary work suits people who work in such fields as health care, business, social care, or education, because these disciplines usually take an integrated, interdisciplinary approach.

Developing the Research Question or Problem

Starting from a relatively broad topic, you will be able to develop a more focused research question or statement of the research problem, whose solution you will be able to find in the process of researching. Qualitative research is fairly open and nondirectional initially and centers on exploration and meaning rather than explanation or search for cause and effect (grounded theory research is an exception). A research question needs an answer; a research problem—similar to a research question—is a dilemma for which a solution is needed but that is not yet available. The problem might be a set of circumstances or conditions that are difficult, puzzling, or tricky in the area of study. The research question or problem needs to be seen in its wider context rather than being divorced from it.

The following short list offers examples of possible research questions from a range of subjects. These are appropriate for the application of a qualitative research approach because they require an in-depth focus on the topic that qualitative methods are able to provide:

- How do local residents feel about mega events such as the World Cup?
- What is the attraction of a singles holiday?

- What are the differences in the customer service offered by service staff of varying nationalities?
- How do tourists respond to seeing poverty during their holiday?

When you have found your potential research question or uncovered a problem, keep in mind the following criteria (adapted from Holloway & Wheeler, 2010):

1. the research must be doable/feasible;
2. the research question and answer to it needs to be relevant and important;
3. the study must be manageable within the timeframe and resources;
4. the topic should be of interest to you and potential readers.

Feasibility

Although philosophical and moral questions might be answerable, they do not usually call for empirical research. However, you might transform a moral dilemma or issue into a research question by rephrasing it so that it can be investigated by exploring participants' ideas and behavior. For instance, this moral question—"is it right or wrong to hate your enemy on the sports field?"—can be rephrased as a specific question and focus on footballers' actions and feelings toward their opponents.

You should also make sure that the data required to answer your research question are obtainable. There is no point in identifying a research problem or question that demands access to people who are hard to reach. Gatekeepers, those who allow access to participants, might impede the progress of research if they are unwilling to allow access, thus access must be considered in advance. One of us remembers a nursing student who had gained permission from the relevant manager, clinical lead, and hospital to carry out a piece of research, but the specialists involved in the direct treatment of patients denied access, so the research could not proceed. Another example involved a student who wished to study tourists' motivations for visiting a garden; he didn't anticipate that access to visitors would be denied by the owners.

> *Find out about access at proposal time; if you cannot get access, you will not be able to start your research as early as you wish—if at all.*

Relevance/Importance

Personal relevance and interest alone are insufficient reasons for choosing a topic, although they may drive the initial choice of topic and help to motivate you during the course of the study. The topic or problem and the solution to it must be relevant and of interest to society, to a professional group, and/or to the academic community. Sometimes relevance and importance lie in the interest of a commissioning agency or firm from which you receive funding, but this situation should not provide the only reason for choosing a topic.

You must ask yourself whether the potential findings of your research will contribute to the essential body of knowledge in the field; this is a question that you will have to answer in your dissertation and during the doctoral defense. Also, you will have to write about relevance in the introductory chapter of your research report, where you state the rationale for your research.

Your study must make an original contribution to knowledge; however, this contribution need not be dramatic or global. If you are a practitioner-researcher, you might consider how your findings will influence your work setting. For instance, if you are a physiotherapist, they might make a difference in the care of patients; if you are a lecturer, they might influence educational practices; if you are a sportsperson, the findings might change coaching behavior. The study should include implications for practice, which will be alluded to in the proposal and in your introduction and drawn out specifically in the final chapter of your dissertation.

Manageability (Doability)

Determine the timeframe and resources at your disposal. Many research problems need a long time span for their solution, but a doctoral dissertation or thesis has to be completed within a few years, and you are generally the sole researcher. Arguably, voluntary participants are one of the most important elements in your research, so you have to take into account the time needed for their recruitment, as well as for the permission of any gate keepers of settings and of access to people and the process of approval by Institutional Review Boards (IRBs) and ethics committees. This is a long process that might involve several steps, and it generally takes longer for qualitative researchers. Moreover, you must look at your own skills and decide whether you have the competence to carry out this doctorate. If they need updating and development, there may be courses at your university that provide this support; otherwise, you might have to improve your skills on your own through the relevant texts on methodology. We have found through our own experience with doctoral candidates that many students developed ambitious and complex research questions that they did not have the competence to address. It is better to carry out a simple study well and in depth rather than complex research badly and in a superficial manner. You need also to develop good time-management skills.

Enthusiasm and Interest

Even before you formulate a research question, you start your work with an interest in the field of study. Researchers generally select a topic and formulate a research question that they are enthusiastic about. If you cannot sustain enthusiasm and interest in the research, you will not complete the thesis. Indeed, your interest in the topic is one of the most important factors in doing a doctorate, because it will help to sustain your motivation over time. Your research also needs to be of interest and relevance to the readers of your study; you do not write for yourself alone.

Changing Your Mind

During the stage of selecting the topic area and finding the research question you will change your mind many times on reflection and in discussion with others, including colleagues and friends, official advisors, and experts in the field. This is a normal part of intellectual development as you progress through the program, and it will give you insight into your topic. Initially there will be many issues and arguments, but eventually you will withdraw from others and make up your own mind. It will, after all, be *your* study. The main advice experienced writers and advisors could give to students is this: *you* will have to justify your choice of topic and your research question to others; therefore *you* must take the final decision on topic and focus.

The Aim of the Research

The research question and aim are often chosen at the same time, although the aim becomes more refined on reflection. The aim reveals your intentions to the readers of your study and tells them what you wish to achieve.

In a recent study on rheumatoid arthritis, North American authors Salt and Peden (2011:14) stated their aim as follows: "to understand the decision-making process that women with rheumatoid arthritis use when deciding to participate in an evidence-based treatment regime."

In the field of market research, an article by Australians Grace, Weaven, and Ross (2010:174) gives as its aim: "to examine gender differences in consumer perceptions of financial retirement planning."

Usually objectives are not needed, because qualitative research is developmental, and so objectives arise in the course of the study. Some institutions do ask students to choose an aim and several objectives, although this is generally perceived to be rather prescriptive for qualitative research. In case you are asked to provide objectives, we include a short definition and example of each. The research aim is a general statement of what is to be achieved overall, an aspiration of the study, whereas an objective is a specific step to achieve the aim. For example:

Aim: The aim of this dissertation is to explore the career paths of hotel managers in the United States.

Objectives:

- To identify managers' roles and functions
- To explore the effect of education on career patterns
- To investigate the career mobility among managers
- To assess the skills perceived as needed for a career in hotel management

A common flaw made in establishing the aim of research, especially by practitioner-researchers, is phrasing it as a solution to a stated problem. For example, a doctorate student investigates bullying in schools and describes the aim: "to develop strategies to avoid bullying in schools." Although this might be the eventual consequence of research, the development of strategies is not a suitable research aim. The aim might be rephrased as: "my aim is to explore the perceptions and behavior of students related to bullying behavior in order to develop strategies for avoiding bullying in schools." The research is about and on bullying behavior, not on strategies. Keep in mind that it is not necessarily your job to solve problems but to investigate an issue that *might* lead to change.

The Timeline

At an early stage of research, you should draw or write a project timeline that fits the type of research you propose to carry out. Some studies need more time than others: for instance, research that requires both interviews and observation often takes longer than does a study with interviews alone. Fieldwork demands familiarization and immersion in the setting, whereas document analysis can be carried out a little faster, although of course both need mindfulness and attention to detail from the researcher. Some students have a more detailed timeline than others do. If events prevent you from keeping to the timeline, it needs to be changed; don't lose sight of the final deadline and the tasks to be completed before then.

When creating a timeline, our students find it useful to work backward from the completion date or deadline for final submission. Take into account how much time you need to prepare for binding and final submission. And time for proofreading the dissertation or thesis is very important, because a well-presented piece of work makes a good impression and produces a halo effect (a positive evaluation that is transferred from one area to another). Make sure that you allow for a final review of the relevant literature toward the end of the research; remember that in qualitative research the literature review is ongoing (see Chapter 6).

The initial phase of the study takes a while, because you need to start reading and then revising your proposal in light of your initial literature review as well as early discussions with advisors. Although these processes are ongoing, they require more effort in the very beginning. Block out holidays or days when you might not be able to work—and allow for unexpected events. Consider what you need to do month by month, allowing time for reading and discussion.

Think also of the practicalities of data collection. As we have mentioned, often access to participants can be gained only through gatekeepers, and this process takes time. Participants need ample notice of when interviews and observations will take place and often are not prepared to be interviewed during their own or their children's holidays. Advisors or supervisors, too, are sometimes unavailable during certain periods in the year. There might also be institutional constraints imposed by your university.

In some qualitative approaches, data collection and analysis interact, and analysis depends on newly acquired data. Because of this, students learn about specific approaches early in their research journey. One example: we have had two students attempt grounded theory (GT), who, without asking for advice, quickly conducted a large number of interviews. Because GT data collection and analysis interact, this was an inappropriate way to go about data collection, and the students had to start over. The interplay between data collection and analysis often occurs in ethnography, too. We learned from this and now remind students at the start of their study to think of the specific strategies and procedures of their approach. The data analysis and the interpretation phases are iterative and take a large chunk of your time.

The times of doctorates vary from university to university, and from country to country, sometimes considerably; Table 2.1 on the next page provides an example. This table does not show that all stages of the work overlap; the literature review is ongoing throughout, and students keep writing during the process. Institutional Review Board or Ethics Committee approval needs to be obtained at an early phase of all doctoral studies.

Usually a few months are allowed for the final write-up, but this is not sufficient for the whole research account; therefore, you should write *all the way through* the research process, so that you do not run out of time at the end. Plan each stage of the process; allow time for reading, writing, and all other tasks.

> *Familiarize yourself with all demands and guidelines of your institution before you set out on the doctoral path.*

Summary of Points Linked to Qualitative Research

- The topic is appropriate for qualitative inquiry if it has been under-researched.
- The research question must not be too narrow.
- The research question or problem, although focused on a specific issue, is open to change during the initial period.
- The research question focuses on meaning rather than measurement.
- Qualitative research generally has a longer timeline than quantitative studies, although students might be constricted by institutional demands.

Table 2.1 Comparison of Dissertation Process in the United States and the United Kingdom

United States	United Kingdom
3 years + depending on university and full-time or part-time status	3 years full-time, 6 years part-time, depending on university
Years 1–2	**Year 1**
Months 1–20	*Months 1–3*
Identify topic	Refine topic and aim in consultation with supervisors
Read literature on topic and approach	Refine proposal
Take courses in preparation for research	Conduct an initial literature overview
Write initial literature review	*Months 4–12*
Months 20–24	Write initial literature review and get familiar with approach
Write proposal	Collect initial data and start analysis
Defend the proposal in front of three approved committee members	Upgrade or transfer to doctoral level in front of two approved internal examiners who will examine the work up to this stage
Year 3	**Year 2**
Months 1–5	*Months 1–7*
Collect data and analyze	Collect primary data and start analysis
Month 6	*Months 5–7*
Refine analysis	Further analysis of data and more data collection, depending on one's approach
Months 7–11	**Year 3**
Write up and proofread	*Months 1–7*
Month 12	Conduct a dialogue with the literature
Submit dissertation	Start a draft of the research account
The final defense is generally in front of five members (the proposal examiners and additional external academics who review the proposal; the number varies among universities)	Get up to date on the literature
	Months 7–9
	Write the final draft of the thesis
	Months 9–12
	Proofread the thesis and submit it to the university
	Viva voce by one or two external and one internal examiner(s)

QUESTIONS AND ANSWERS

Question: *I am determined to write a qualitative study but my advisors wish me to use the mixed methods approach. How do I proceed?*

Answer: Find out from your advisors why they want you to use this type of methodology. They might believe that your research question merits an approach different from the one you proposed. If your are determined to write a qualitative doctorate, rephrase your research problem in order to answer a qualitative research question. (See also questions in Chapter 3.)

Question: *I don't think I can complete my study in the allotted time span. What can I do about this?*

Answer: Try to refine your area of research. Simplify the process or use a different approach. Formulate a less complex research question. If during the course of your studies you have personal problems, including illness, your academic institution may be able to defer your hand-in date or suspend your studies temporarily.

Question: *My advisors don't seem to know about qualitative research. What can be done?*

Answer: If you can't find someone at your university, search for experts in qualitative research at a different institution; if your advisors are not acquainted with or sympathetic to qualitative research, you may run into problems. Think about changing advisors.

Question: *My topic is interesting to me. How do I know it's important enough in my field?*

Answer: Conduct an initial literature review so that you can determine if the topic has been covered before. During this review, you should also discover what areas of research practitioners and academics regard as important; it will be useful if you can say that you are responding to a call for research.

Question: *How long should I be prepared to spend on reading about my chosen approach?*

Answer: If you have not used the identified approach before, be prepared to spend a few months reading the relevant literature on research methods so that you are familiar with the theoretical, philosophical, and historical underpinnings associated with the approach as well as with the methods you need to use. This will save much time later on; the more prepared you are for the primary data collection phase the better.

Question: *I have identified a research question, but I cannot seem to formulate an aim. I am interested in how marketing manipulates the unconscious, but I don't know who my participants will be and what questions I would ask them to arrive at an answer to my question.*

Answer: In this case, you might need to abandon the proposed research; even at proposal stage and especially during primary data-collection stage, you will probably find it difficult and time-consuming to identify the route to answering your research question, which is interesting to you but empirically challenging, if not impossible, to investigate.

Question: *I intend to study part-time. How do I modify the timeline?*

Answer: Look at each year and determine what you will be able to do. It might be a good idea to go backward from the point of submission.

Question: *If I study part-time, how long will the data be useful?*

Answer: It depends whether the data will stay important for a while. Most data will be useful for a few years. It is, however, important not to prolong the study beyond "the sell-by date" of the data.

Question: *Writing a qualitative doctoral dissertation sounds like an enormous commitment. Any tips how I can ensure staying on track and motivated?*

Answer: This is why we suggest choosing a topic that is of interest to you. Form discussion groups with others who have the same concerns, give presentations at conferences, talk about your research, and get feedback.

3. Selecting a Research Approach

This is not a method text; hence we can offer here only a short overview of some of the most popular approaches. At the end of the book we supply a brief list of key reading so that you can learn more about the approach in which you are interested. (For a fuller account read also Creswell, 2007 or Richards & Morse, 2007.)

In this chapter we cover the key principles and characteristics of four popular approaches; however, others exist, such as discourse analysis, action research, and performative social science approaches.

> *Choose from the range of qualitative approaches that best fit your research and aim.*

Ethnography

The aim of ethnography is to describe and interpret a particular cultural setting with all the similarities and diversities of the people in this setting. *Ethnography,* first used in anthropological research, refers to the description of a group, culture, or community, and it traditionally remains the approach associated with anthropology. The goal of *anthropology,* which derives from the Greek *anthropos* meaning "man" or "human," and *logos,* meaning "thought" or "reason," is to describe social behavior, with the principle of studying it in an everyday setting. Ethnography requires you, the researcher, to become immersed in the field, with extended periods

Essentials of a Qualitative Doctorate by Immy Holloway and Lorraine Brown, 39–47

of fieldwork enabling you to become accepted within the research setting. Your physical presence in the field allows you to gain firsthand experience of the group under study and to be spontaneous and instrumental in terms of what type of data you collect, and when. People are therefore studied in everyday settings, interacting as they would normally do, with minimal interference and influence from the researcher (Brewer, 2000).

Ethnographers have a long-term engagement with a group: time enables relationships to develop and permits the observation of detail and processes, rather than a static image captured at certain points (O'Reilly, 2011). However, a shorter period of immersion in the setting has become increasingly acceptable. For doctoral students there is always time pressure, and sometimes you will find that you don't spend as long a time in a setting as you would like, or should. However, you do need prolonged engagement with the setting, the duration of which you need to discuss with your advisors and justify.

Culture is used as the central organizing concept of anthropology (Spradley, 1979), and *ethnography*, which similarly derives from the Greek (*ethnos*, "nation"; *graphein*, "writing"), means *the writing of culture*. Ethnography then is the description, interpretation, and portrayal of a culture or social group through thick description (see Chapter 1). The term *ethnography* refers to both the study of unfamiliar cultures and to the study of subcultures within your own society. This type of ethnography has been described as "anthropology at home." Two advantages of dealing with subcultures are that there is no alien tongue to master and the culture of interest is partially known at the outset of study. Ethnographers attempt to make the familiar strange, questioning their own preconceptions.

Ethnographic data collection occurs mainly through participant observation of behavior and interactions. Observation involves collecting data from the culture under study, because observers who become or are already part of the culture take note of everything they see and hear. Although groups or cultures have many shared values, norms and rituals, the people within it have often different perceptions and beliefs depending on their location in the culture. Ethnographers adopt the emic perspective, seeing the culture from the inside (see Chapter 1). Observations are the starting point for interviews with cultural members. Some interviews are formal and planned, but you may often ask questions on the spur of the moment, taking advantage of opportunistic conversations. Ethnographers also keep an ethnographic record; from the beginning you should record what goes on in the field of the local culture or subculture under study (Gobo, 2008).

Critical ethnography is a type of ethnography that focuses on social factors such as power and control (Madison, 2005; Thomas, 1993). It often aims to change the status quo and bring about change. Auto-ethnography (Reed-Danahay, 1997) is a branch of ethnography that seems popular with students. It focuses on the feelings and experiences of the researchers themselves. Although it is a legitimate way of doing research, you need to avoid self-absorption, and to relate your own experiences to those of others.

Netnography, a term used by Robert Kozinets in the 1990s, is a way of carrying out ethnographic inquiry on the internet, particularly in consumer research. This has become ever more popular in recent years as it saves researchers traveling to observe and interview participants. Although the catchy name has caught on, it is similar to other types of research on the net. Internet research involves the same disadvantages and advantages of non-face-to-face interviews and observations. (To learn more about this, see Kozinets, 2010; Mann & Stewart, 2000.)

Phenomenology

The aim of phenomenological research is to describe and interpret the meaning of people's experiences and their life-world, both at an individual unique and at a general level. Phenomenology originated as an approach to philosophy and was only later developed as a method of inquiry. For an overview, you might consult the reader on phenomenology by Moran (2000). The goal of phenomenological research is to describe a *phenomenon* as it manifests itself to consciousness. For Giorgi and Giorgi (2003), phenomenology is the study of consciousness, it describers the essential structure of experience (essence).

There are several approaches in phenomenology. Each has different ways of conducting phenomenological research although their aims are similar. Phenomenological research is mainly divided into two main types that have some common but also several distinctive features: descriptive phenomenology and interpretive or hermeneutic phenomenology. Within the latter branch, interpretative phenomenological analysis (IPA) is now popular. Either approach can be used, but you must ensure that you preserve the integrity of the particular approach you choose.

Descriptive phenomenology was translated into an empirical research approach by Amedeo Giorgi who sought to develop a rigorous descriptive empirical phenomenology inspired by Husserlian philosophy. The major aim of a descriptive phenomenological research approach is to generate a description of a phenomenon of everyday experience and to identify its essential structure. Data sources are interviews and narratives of participants and anything else that describes the lived experience of participants.

Hermeneutics or interpretive phenomenological research on the other hand prioritizes understanding over description and is interpretive, thus Heidegger's phenomenology, which moved the phenomenological project beyond description to interpretation, is paramount. A weakness of hermeneutic phenomenology is that there is a lack of guidelines for students to follow; though Van Manen (1998) proposes six research steps, you will find that they are not prescriptive. In hermeneutic phenomenology researchers go beyond description to interpretation.

Because of its simple guidelines, *interpretative phenomenological research* (*IPA*) is often chosen by students. Developed by Jonathan Smith in the 1990s with others, this hermeneutic method stresses the interpretation of data (Smith, Flowers, & Larkin, 2009). The data sources consist of interviews, but other data can also be used. IPA focuses on the way participants make sense of their experiences. Although each case is looked at individually, researchers also seek patterns across these cases (Finlay, 2011). As in other phenomenological approaches, the sample size is usually small.

Common to all phenomenology is the concept of bracketing. Bracketing involves suspending beliefs and prior assumptions about a phenomenon in order properly to examine what is present, to describe the "essence" of things. For Husserl, this was at the center of his understanding of the practice of phenomenology, calling this suspension of preconceptions "the phenomenological reduction," which aims for open-mindedness in researchers. This does not mean that you try to empty yourself of all past knowledge but that you put this knowledge aside. Both descriptive and hermeneutic phenomenologists would agree that the possibility of seeing something freshly, differently, or from a new perspective is a crucial dimension of phenomenology's discovery-oriented approach. At the core of phenomenological study is the notion of the life-world (*Lebenswelt*), also known as "lived experience." Aspers (2004) suggests that researchers do not study an objectively existing reality but a phenomenologically experienced world. Thus you should focus on everyday lived experience, seeking to elicit from your participants a concrete detailed description of their experiences (Giorgi, 1997) in interviews which start with a request that they fully describe a relevant experience linked to particular phenomena. Phenomenological research generates findings that go beyond individual cases to the more general. This move from the individual to the universal is known as the eidetic reduction.

Grounded Theory

The aim of grounded theory (GT) is to develop a theory of how people make sense of their world in interaction with others. This research approach was first developed by Glaser and Strauss in their foundational text published in 1967. There are many versions of GT, in particular the Straussian perspective which Strauss developed with Corbin, and that of Glaser (1992 and later publications) who criticized this as divergent from the original meaning of their original text. A third version has recently emerged, the constructivist grounded theory of Charmaz (2006), which is often used by students.

GT is a popular approach for those who wish to develop theory, examine a process, or modify an existing theory. It is also useful for examining interactions between social actors or trajectories—movements of change over time. GT differs from other qualitative approaches in that it is explanatory, but explanations are always rooted in evidence from the data (hence *grounded* theory). Indeed, the goal of the grounded theorist is to move beyond description and to generate theory directly and systematically from the data. It is not always possible for researchers to develop a completely new or original theory; they may instead make modifications to an established theory, and this is legitimate. The emphasis on theory building makes it one of the more complex approaches. However its use in generating theory where it is lacking makes it often an obvious choice.

Distinctive to GT is the iterative nature of research; you will find that data collection and analysis interact and proceed simultaneously. The incoming data from observations, interviews, and other data sources generate ideas during the analysis which in turn will guide you in the collection of further data. The *initial* sample might be small; further sampling depends on the data you have previously collected and analyzed. Data collection and analysis interact and generate concepts, and these determine your decision as to where to go next. This is known as theoretical sampling which is made on the basis of concepts that arise in the research and which are then followed up by collecting and analyzing further data. Important to GT is also the concept of theoretical saturation that occurs when no new ideas *important for the developing theory* arise. This is not to suggest that no new data are generated in primary research but that the data might not be of relevance to the main theory under development or the agenda of the researcher.

Once saturation has been reached, and data have been coded and categorized, and incidents for each category are compared (constant comparison), you generate or discover the core category. This core category develops the storyline which integrates all elements of the emergent theory. Thus the core category can only be fully developed on completion of the research. The theory must have explanatory power.

Narrative Research

Narrative research, or narrative analysis (Riessman, 1993, 2008), has as its aim the exploration of participants' stories about their feelings and thoughts about an experience or a phenomenon. It is defined by Holloway and Freshwater (2007:4) as "a verbal or written representation of events or experiences expressed in a way that can be understood by others." Narration is viewed by the authors as an integral and universal part of human nature: people have a natural desire to share stories and to communicate; meaning emerges through the act of story-telling. The term *narrative* or *story* is also used to refer to creative writing, but in academic research, narrative inquiry refers to data collected by researchers for a specific purpose. You can elicit stories for the purposes of a specific inquiry or you can analyse accounts that are naturally, produced for some purpose other than research.

Narrative research accounts may be told by participants in a chaotic, iterative and non-linear manner, and it is your job to retell the story in a coherent way. The story is always about something, it should have a plot (or theme), a pattern of events, often a problem, and sometimes subplots which enrich the plot. The story carries moments of tension, which are relieved at the end of telling. The lead role in the account is usually the story-teller, but other characters in the story told by both the participant and the researcher should be brought to life; the account must be interesting and believable.

Narrative research uses the "the experiences as expressed in lived and told stories of individuals" (Creswell, 2007:4), usually in the form of verbal or written accounts. The narrative data for your project are generated from participants in one to one meetings, often over several hours. You should be prepared to spend a considerable amount of time with the participants.

Participants are encouraged to talk about their experience in an uninterrupted flow, thus giving them more power to guide the research. Semistructured interviews interrupt participants and "fracture the text"

limitation

(Riessman, 1993), whereas narrative interviewing preserves the holistic nature of the story. Narrative interviews require minimum intervention, and only a few trigger questions are needed.

Narrative data can be analyzed in a number of ways, but the most favored by students and researchers is thematic analysis, because it is more straightforward. The attention focuses on the contents, on what is in the story, rather than how it is told, to whom and for what reasons (Riessman, 2008:54). Narrative research is best used for capturing the detailed stories or life experiences of one person or a small group of participants.

You should remember that your final account—the dissertation or journal article—is also a narrative. "Re-storying" reorganizes data so that plot, character, chronology, and place are clear.

Commonalities between Qualitative Approaches

You will find more commonalities between these approaches than differences. Data sources include interviews, observation, and documents, but others are also included, such as documents, diaries, and visual data. Phenomenological and narrative approaches do not generally involve participant observation. Often the types of analysis have similarities but they can also be distinguished from one another. (See the list of key texts at the end of the book.)

> *The chosen approach should be consistent with the research question, data collection, sampling, and analysis so that the study will become coherent and sound.*

Approaches differ in terms of data collection, analysis, and presentation. Once you have chosen the most suitable approach, spend some time reading about it and its associated procedures so that you uphold the integrity of the particular approach you adopt. Many times we have witnessed students getting into trouble at the examination stage of the doctoral journey when they haven't followed important methodological principles. Once you are familiar with the key literature on your chosen approach, you can start to plan data collection. You will find that the research methods' texts associated with your approach will provide you with many handy tips on data management, collection, and analysis. The more prepared you are, the better your experience of doing research will be. Your advisor will discuss your choice of research approach with you, but if you don't select wisely and need or want to change later, it will be difficult to do so. It is a good idea to try to frame your question within each of the major approaches to see which is most likely to fit and answer the question or solve the problem you wish to investigate.

QUESTIONS AND ANSWERS

Question: *I would like to include two approaches to research, such as grounded theory and phenomenology. Can I do this?*

Answer: Although you might have seen this done occasionally, it is not advisable to use two different approaches in one study. Each qualitative approach has its own coherence, underlying ideas and different procedures, and it might be very challenging for you to conform to two different approaches within one study; coherence might be lost, and the account may become confusing. If you choose to do a mixed method design, you are almost carrying out two studies; if you do a multiple methods design, you are doing two studies too. Do you ever want to complete your doctorate? The trick in choosing a dissertation topic is to find one the right size: Can it be done in the time available, with the resources at hand and within your area of expertise and knowledge?

Question: *I'm not sure which approach to take. I keep changing my mind. What if I start and then find the chosen method too difficult?*

Answer: Be careful in the very beginning and read thoroughly around the various ways of doing research. Once you have really made up your mind, do stick to the chosen approach otherwise you waste time. Even if the approach is a difficult one, you will be able to master it after careful study.

Question: *I would like to use GT, but I find the terminology confusing and am unsure as to what constant comparison and saturation mean in practical terms: should I choose an easier approach even though GT suits my topic and aim?*

Answer: If GT is the most appropriate choice of research approach, we would advise to immerse yourself in the approach and read around it and its origins. You will be surprised at how quickly you will become familiar with the associated terminology and procedures. We would also advise you to identify other researchers who have used GT, irrespective of their topic and aim, who will be able to offer advice on common pitfalls, and to read dissertations that have used a GT approach. In other words, your concerns will be overcome if you dedicate time at the beginning of the study to familiarization with the approach.

Question: *I understand that I should spend a long time in the field if I am using an ethnographic approach; however, the event I wish to research is the FIFA World Cup 2018, which has a duration of only six weeks. I am worried that this will be regarded as too short a time span.*

Answer: Although it is true that anthropologists advise researchers to spend at least a year immersed in the research setting, there has been an increased tendency to spend less time in immersion for similar reasons to those cited above. You need to discuss why ethnography is the right approach for you, to show that you understand the disadvantages of spending less time than is traditional in the setting and to describe how you will strive to become as familiar as possible with the culture under observation.

Question: *I am attracted to a particular research method (I attended a specialist conference). Rather than start with a topic area, can I start with a preferred method and find the appropriate research question?*

Answer: Many advisors would tell you not to do this. We think, however, that it is acceptable, especially if it will keep you interested. You will usually find a research question or problem in your discipline or work that can be answered by using your chosen method. Discuss this with your advisor.

4. Proposal Writing

Before the research starts, you need to write a proposal and, for obvious reasons, consider the literature, so that you can demonstrate that there is demand for the research (see Chapter 3). All doctoral dissertation proposals will be presented to a review panel or a research committee for evaluation and permission to proceed. Even though you might be familiar with proposal writing, read other candidates' qualitative research proposals to gain an idea of what yours might look like, and also to avoid mistakes.

Ask the relevant university department for good previous qualitative proposals so that you can become familiar with the style. When you are writing, remember that the study will be an academic and scientific document and not just an empirical piece of research for the purpose of gaining a grant. Many educational institutions have guidelines for writing a proposal, although not necessarily for qualitative studies.

What Is a Proposal?

The proposal is the plan and justification for your research that you present to your advisors, review committee, and/or to a funding body. Because qualitative inquiry evolves *during* the research process, the qualitative proposal differs from the quantitative; it is less static and fixed. When you present the proposal to your review committee and advisors you might suggest that the plan could change over time depending on the direction the research takes during its early stages. Indeed, most review committees and advisors know about this potential for change, but it's advisable to show that you know about qualitative research.

Essentials of a Qualitative Doctorate by Immy Holloway and Lorraine Brown, 49–56
© 2012 Left Coast Press, Inc. All rights reserved.

The proposal consists—more or less—of a summary of the three sections of the study: the introduction, methodology, and initial literature review. However, the qualitative proposal differs from the quantitative in its broader approach to a research problem and in the overview of the literature, which is not comprehensive and is less detailed (see Chapter 6). Kilbourn (2006:536) stresses that in the proposal "straightforward clarity about what, why, how, who, and when is critical."

Be aware that academic institutions differ in their guidelines about the length and breadth of the research proposal. In our university, for instance, doctoral candidates have the opportunity to submit an initial proposal that can be short, and after about six months they are expected to present a more detailed proposal, which is written with some help from their advisors.

Steps in the Proposal

The proposal is generally written in a well-organized and structured sequence. When you start your proposal, write as though you are explaining the study to a person who doesn't know very much about your area or topic; this approach will force you to be explicit. You can later revise the written text if you feel it is too simplistic. Keep in mind some of the advice from Chapter 2: if the study isn't feasible, relevant, or interesting, it will not find favor with your readers.

The proposal generally includes these steps:

1. Working title
2. Abstract
3. Introduction to the topic area
   Problem statement and aim
   Rationale (justification)
   Context and background
   Limitations and boundaries
4. Initial literature review
5. Methodology and methods
   Justification for the qualitative approach
   Methods (such as data sources, collection, and analysis)
   Sampling (including access)
   Ethical issues
6. Plan of the journey/the timeline
7. Researcher's credentials

(The importance of the title and abstract is covered in Chapter 10.)

1. Working Title

The title of the study is provisional and might change during the research process; hence it is called "working title." At our university, students must give a permanent title to the study when stating their "intention to submit" the final dissertation, but other places demand a fixed title at registration or at an early stage. Make sure of your university's regulations. Sometimes you will be allowed to change a permanent title, but you will have to get official permission for this. Don't give an overlong title (no more than 16 words or so), but make it clear and precise, reflecting the essence of the study. If you have too many words, segment it into a title and a subtitle.

Titles (Real and Invented)

- Making Sense of Classroom Interaction
- Achieving Normality: Status Passage to Motherhood after a Caesarean Section
- Gender, Class, and "Binge" Drinking: An Ethnography of Southtown's Night-Time Economy (*Southtown is a pseudonym.*)

You can see that these examples start with key words that note the essence of the research. Many writers point out that phrases such as "an exploration of," "an investigation into," and "aspects of" are redundancies and should be omitted (see, for instance, Locke, Spirduso, & Silverman, 2007).

2. Abstract

The abstract is a brief description or summary of the proposed work; it should describe the aim of your work and its rationale in brief, as well as the methods that you intend to use, including a sample. As you can see, abstracts are about the what, why, and how. The proposal abstract is written in the future tense, because you have not yet carried out the research. In the final dissertation, you will, of course, convert the abstract to the past tense.

3. Introduction

In the introduction to your area of potential study, the research problem or question must be clearly stated so that readers can assess whether your research will be relevant and worthwhile. The important concepts related to this area will form some of the staging points in your journey, when you take stock and reflect on them. Here you will locate the rationale or justification for your work: why are you doing it, and why is it needed in your discipline or area? Reviewers assess whether you are contributing to knowledge in your area of study and whether this contribution differs from those of others. The aim of the research must be clearly stated (see Chapter 2). Some researchers do this after the initial literature review, since the aim is a direct outcome of a demonstrated gap in the research; others state it at the very beginning of the proposal. *Specific* steps (objectives) to reach the aim will develop during the research rather than in the beginning, but some institutions will require you to include objectives in the proposal. The overarching aim generally refers to an understanding of participants' feelings, to participants' experiences of or perspectives on a phenomenon in a particular context and setting, and to studying participants' behaviors in a specific setting.

> - The aim of my research is to examine the phenomenon of pain from the perspective of people suffering from chronic back pain.
> - The aim of the study is to explore the lifeworld of international students at American universities.

The setting—the physical location, environment, and context—and the circumstances and conditions in which the study takes place should be included in this section; these are important details in qualitative research, because findings are always context-bound. A short description of your own stance and background should also be included; you are aware and acknowledge that the researcher is the main tool of qualitative research and therefore has an important influence on its conduct (reflexivity). The boundaries that limit your research (the delimitations) need a short description, as do the potential limitations of the research—that is, the weaknesses that might affect the outcome of your research and how they can be overcome. These issues should be included in the introduction and the methodology sections, depending on whether they are related to topic area or methods.

4. Initial Literature Review

This review (as outlined in the first part of Chapter 6) describes and critiques related studies in the field and places your study in the context of other people's writing and research. The readers of the proposal should see how your study will be different from those of previous researchers but also how it will contribute to the broad dialogue in the research area. The literature review will, you hope, convince the reader that your work is needed and will advance knowledge. Qualitative researchers contextualize their research by locating it in time and environment; therefore, you should situate your research in its contemporary sociocultural context.

5. Methodology and Methods

The proposal needs to include justification for the use of qualitative methodology and the specific approach that you are considering. Be aware that the rationale for qualitative research might be longer than that for a traditional quantitative study, because members of ethics and review committees might be less familiar with qualitative inquiry. The method section describes how you are going to carry out your research, as well as which sources of data you will use and how you will collect them (that is, interviews, observation, and so on). You should also cover the type of data analysis, be it phenomenological, grounded theory, narrative, and so on. Demonstrate that you understand the different types of analysis available, and make sure that you use some references for methodology and approach in the proposal.

You must also discuss the sampling strategy you will use. Sampling in qualitative research is criterion-based and purposeful, and its makeup depends on the purpose for which it is used; for instance, in health research your sample might include individuals who have a similar condition; in sport research, a group of people who are fans or participants in a particular sport; in market research, a group of people at whom a product is directed. Remember to cite inclusion and exclusion criteria for participants (for instance, you might wish to exclude certain individuals such as vulnerable people or young children). Remember that the purposive sample is not always predetermined in qualitative inquiry; it evolves. People and other sampling units can be added, your choice influenced by concepts that emerge from your research (this is *theoretical sampling*). Sampling issues might become problematic when you present your proposal to a review or ethics committee who might wish to receive firm ideas about sampling from you, so you should be able to defend your sampling strategy. It is also a good idea to tell the reader of your proposal how you intend to gain access to your participants.

Also make sure that ethical issues receive proper discussion (see Chapter 5). You need to show that participation in the research is voluntary, that you will protect participants from risk and harm, and that confidentiality and anonymity will be ensured.

6. Plan/Timeline

Academic institutions generally ask for a detailed timeline or time scale for the research. All are keen for their doctoral students to complete in record time, and they want to be convinced that you have good time-management skills and are realistic about the tasks in front of you. Transcription, analysis, and interpretation are time-consuming tasks, and this fact should be reflected in your timeline. Most universities have cut-off dates for doctoral studies; but you should also try to keep to the deadlines you have set for yourself.

7. Researcher's Credentials (Proposal)

A section on your credentials as a researcher shows whether you have the skills and knowledge to complete your doctorate. You should show an acquaintance with the research approach that you intend to use as well as some familiarity with the topic and the discipline in which it is located. Your first degree, your Masters, and other recent qualifications or courses in the area of your proposed research will strengthen your credentials and the chance that the proposal will find acceptance by its assessors.

Inclusion of Theoretical Perspectives

The theoretical grounding in a qualitative dissertation is different from that in quantitative research. Whereas the latter is often rooted in established theory, much qualitative inquiry generates or modifies theory from the findings of the research. Nevertheless, theoretical ideas become part of the study from the very beginning, because established theory contributes to most academic and scholarly research. For instance, grounded theorists often base their studies in symbolic interactionism, whereas ethnographers firmly ground their research in ideas about culture. However, in the proposal you will not be able to develop major theoretical perspectives of your research.

A good proposal will convince the review or research degree committee that

- the research question will contribute to knowledge in the field;
- the aim of the research is achievable;
- the doctoral candidate understands the issues involved in the research, be they topic or method related.

Even at this early stage, when writing your proposal you will need to be reflexive—aware of your assumptions based on your knowledge, background, and experiences and able to acknowledge and confront them.

Summary

- The proposal reflects the flexibility of qualitative research; the research might change over time.
- Although researchers need a good grasp of the topic and area of the research, they need to state the possibility for change of direction.
- Sampling issues are ongoing and cannot be wholly determined in the proposal.

QUESTIONS AND ANSWERS

Question: *My proposal committee might identify weaknesses in my research proposal. How will I defend my study?*

Answer: You might admit that the proposal has developmental weaknesses and that you will use committee members' expertise to address them. Such candor is seen as strength in a researcher, but you might also stress the elements in the proposal that you think are strong.

Question: *My advisors wish for the research to be more prescriptive. How can I address this request?*

Answer: You might reply that qualitative research is known for its flexibility and that your research will become more focused as time passes.

Question: *I don't know exactly at this stage who my participants will be; how can I cover sampling in the proposal?*

Answer: Although your sample selection may evolve, still indicate on the proposal whom you might target; this shows thought and preparation. Of course, your advisors will understand that your strategy may change.

Question: *I would like to adopt ethnography as an approach, but I am aware that I have to do a lot of reading about the approach before I start to collect data. Will it count against me if my proposal betrays insufficient knowledge of how to do ethnographic research?*

Answer: You should read enough about your approach to write the proposal; in your timeline you can show that you will dedicate two or three months to immersion in the literature on ethnography. The review committee will be pleased that you intend to give so much time to preparation.

Question: *I have been told that I should indicate the theoretical framework that I wish to adopt. Do I have to include this?*

Answer: Although it is common for quantitative researchers to identify a theoretical framework that guides the research, this is not the norm among qualitative researchers, who tend to adopt a more inductive approach to research. You can either defend your decision not to include such a framework, with reference to the qualitative research literature, or, if pushed, include such a framework, which you state will/may be modified by your findings.

Question: *If my proposal was not good enough, can I change it to be reviewed again?*

Answer: Unless it is abysmally bad, the answer is yes, of course.

5. The Importance of Ethical Issues

Before you start your research you must consider ethical issues, which are integral to all studies. This necessity is not just about satisfying ethical review boards and committees but about behaving ethically. Furthermore, ethical considerations continue *throughout* the research process.

> *The field of ethics is related to moral principles as well as rules and standards. Ethical behavior is sensitive to social and cultural contexts and differences and is an integral issue in the research.*

Ethics concerns autonomy, rights, safety, and the well-being of participants. You need to think early on about gaining access to participants and the ethical issues that might arise in the process of your study. In qualitative research in particular, you will not always be able to foresee the ethical problems and dilemmas before you start—especially if you are carrying out your study in the field of healthcare—but you might consider some of the issues that could arise from your specific question and choice of participants. University codes of ethics and the guidelines of review boards and ethics committees are linked

Essentials of a Qualitative Doctorate by Immy Holloway and Lorraine Brown, 57–67
© 2012 Left Coast Press, Inc. All rights reserved.

to the protection of participants and their rights to confidentiality and ano-nymity. Ethical principles have their origin in biomedical research, but many can be applied also to social inquiry (van den Hoonaard, 2008).

The Framework for Research Ethics of the Economic and Social Research Council of Britain (ESRC, 2010:3) established six key principles, concerned with:

- ensuring "integrity, quality, and transparency";
- supplying full information about the aim and uses of the research;
- ensuring confidentiality and anonymity;
- organizing voluntary participation free from coercion;
- avoiding harm to participants;
- guaranteeing the independence of the research and researcher.

These ethical guidelines apply to all research, but there are some that particularly concern qualitative research and have different implications for its conduct (discussed in later sections of this chapter). Of course, you should also consult the latest guidelines of your discipline on ethics con-cerning human participants.

A Step-by-Step Approach

When you are considering the ethical implications of your research, we advise following these steps:

- Gain access to the setting and permission from gatekeepers.
- Inform potential participants about the aims and type of research in which they might be involved.
- Ask participants whether they wish to be involved in the study after they are ensured anonymity and confidentiality.

In this chapter we discuss these and other important issues linked to ethi-cal behavior and highlight those that are specific to qualitative research.

Gaining Access

Gatekeepers such as managers or senior staff in organizations have the power to allow access to participants. This situation in itself might pre-sent a dilemma for you: participants might feel obliged to take part in the research if their superiors have suggested it; hence their participation is not truly voluntary, and the data might become skewed.

Ethical Dilemmas in Gatekeeping

- A doctoral student who works in a country in the Middle East wished to carry out a grounded theory study. She asked senior managers to allow her access to employees in an organization, and permission was granted. When she finally started to interview, she found out that managers had suggested to potential participants that it was in their interest to take part in the research and imperative not to criticize the organization. The candidate had to abandon the site in which she wished to do her research and search for another.
- A student asked a tour operator for access to tourists for an ethnography; this was granted, but the participants were reluctant and unfriendly. The student's experience of observing the trip was uncomfortable, because participants were clearly unhappy about being observed and were unwilling to be interviewed. The data collected were skewed by her presence as a researcher, and so a new site was chosen.

Normally you will be expected to have approval for your study from all involved—gatekeepers, participants, and review boards. Some universities have ethics checklists to be completed by students and signed by their advisors.

The Principle of Autonomy: Voluntary, Informed Participation

As stated by Beauchamp and Childress (2008), voluntary, free, and non-pressured participation is necessary for the research to be ethical. Research participants should be fully informed about the research, give their agreement to take part in it, and be allowed to refuse participation. They can, of course, withdraw at any time during the study. Voluntary informed consent shows respect for autonomy—one of the principles of ethics that every human being should be granted (Gillon, 2003).

Note that, in the process of gaining consent, it is difficult to give exact information to prospective participants in qualitative research. First, the research might change because of its flexibility, and so detailed objec tives are difficult to establish at the very beginning. Second, if you give very detailed and full information, you might skew the research, because the participant may just tell you what you want to hear; however, the goal of qualitative research is to pursue the perspectives and/or behavior of participants. Of course, you will need to have an overall agenda, and the participant should be informed as much as is appropriate and possible. By the end of the research, participants should be in a position to make a decision as to the use of the data they have supplied. Furthermore, as indicated by Morse and colleagues (2008), consent should be obtained on a regular basis *throughout* the research: it should not be a one-time event.

Institutional review boards and ethics committees often expect written consent from all involved participants and gatekeepers. Sometimes, however, this may have a negative effect on the research and could be inappropriate (Green & Thorogood, 2009; van den Hoonaard, 2008). Individuals are sometimes reluctant to sign forms and might reconsider their involvement if required to do so. If at all possible, do gain written consent from your participants.

Anonymity and Confidentiality

You need to reassure participants that you won't reveal their identity, thus guaranteeing anonymity. This sounds easy but can become problematic—for example, you might inadvertently or indirectly disclose a person's identity in a detailed job description or in stating the age, gender, and nationality of the participant.

> - A doctoral candidate in marketing communications interviewed an individual within a particular occupation with a specific job title. The researcher realized that only one person in the area had this title, so this detail, which contextualized the data, had to be omitted from the final account.
> - A student undertaking a doctorate in health research observed a number of people who had problems with their kidney transplant in interaction with health professionals. Only one man was involved in this group of patients. He was left out of the research account (even though it might have been interesting and valuable to include him) for fear of readers identifying him.
> - In an interview, a participant raised sensitive issues about life in her country. She could have been traced by readers of the research report, because not many people of her nationality were studying in the U.K. town mentioned at that time, and reprisals might be carried out because of her revelations. The researcher decided to exclude the important insights she offered in a bid to protect the participant's identity and to keep her from harm, even though the participant insisted that she didn't mind if she were identified.

To avoid identification of participants you can use pseudonyms and change ages slightly (say, by two years). If you change ages, you need to do this consistently throughout your table—for instance, change everybody's age by two years—and you cannot divulge the exact number of years by which you have changed their age. Participants might also be given numbers or letters in the research account (for instance, Participant H, Participant 7), although this is rather impersonal. Pseudonyms are livelier and enhance the storyline. Memos and fieldnotes should also be devoid of personal identifiers, because they might fall into the wrong hands.

The name of the institution or location might have to be changed, too, especially if participants do not wish to disclose it. Before starting the study you should consider the course of action you would take should your findings be disclosed and they are unfavorable to participants or to an organization; discuss the latter possibility with the gatekeepers before you start.

- A study of the incidence of racism against international students in a town in the United Kingdom might endanger international student recruitment and thereby the financial health of the town and of the institution. And yet the findings were significant; advice was taken and care was made not to reveal the identity of the town and the institution.
- An organizational sociologist and doctoral candidate carries out research in a business organization. The research is highly critical of the firm in which the study takes place. After reviewing the research, the senior members of the firm are willing for the findings to be published but insist on the identity of the firm being withheld to avoid harming their business. The researcher respects their wishes.

Confidentiality is another problematic issue in qualitative inquiry, and it is closely linked to privacy. Of course, confidential data must not be disclosed to the public. However, in the findings chapters of your dissertation, you will want to give evidence from the data. Using quotations helps to liven up the discussion, but their use can lead to a breach in confidentiality. So, you must consider how you will maintain your promise of anonymity and confidentiality. Doctoral advisors will be able to see the data (but they are, of course, aware of confidentiality issues). If you use transcribers, they also need to be advised of confidentiality; and be careful not to disclose private matters inadvertently to friends or colleagues.

> In a study of the influence of gender on completing a doctorate, transcription was undertaken by a third party who worked with both the researchers and the participants. In this case, a statement was completed and signed that ensured the anonymity and confidentiality of data. Participants were also asked if they were comfortable with transcription being carried out by one of their colleagues.

Participants must be informed of the involvement of others who might see the data, and they should be asked to give their permission for this. Furthermore, you must not divulge information that participants wish to keep completely private.

> - In a study of international student adjustment, a Chinese student told of an experience of racism that took place at the university. She asked the researcher not to report this, and the promise not to do so had to be kept despite the researcher's desire to make the member of staff concerned accountable for his/her actions.
> - The use of a digital or video recorder presents specific dilemmas. First of all, participants need to be comfortable with recordings and reassured that these will not fall into the wrong hands. Second, transcriptions and fieldnotes must be kept secure and should not be stored near the recordings. Patton (2002) suggests that recordings should be erased shortly after the research, but many universities or funding agencies wish them to be kept for a number of years. However, only the researcher should be able to match real names and identities with any records kept, and participants should be given numbers or pseudonyms in the research account.

The Principles of Nonmaleficence and Beneficence: Doing No Harm and Doing Good

The principle of nonmaleficence, "first, do no harm," demands that no harm will come to the participants through the research. Any risk to them will have to be carefully assessed and as far as possible eliminated (see also the section on interviews and observation). The rights, autonomy, and dignity of all participants must be protected. Also the researcher should "do good" if possible; there should be positive benefit for the individual or society (the principle of beneficence).

- An experienced mental health nurse wished to study the effects of suicide on people whose parents or partners had committed suicide. Her research was approved by the relevant ethics committee, but she felt early in the study that her participants were hurt—possibly harmed—by bringing back memories of a painful time in their lives. She abandoned the research.
- In a study on culture shock, many participants cried during interviews, and this made the researcher concerned that she was disturbing them, even though they said that they found the chance to speak about themselves therapeutic. She made a commitment to follow up on their welfare after the interviews.

Justice, Fairness, and Reciprocity

Research strategies and procedures must be fair, not only taking into account the equality of human beings but also respecting their diversity (such as gender, age, ethnic group, disability). This principle can be restated simply as "equals should be treated equally and unequals unequally," a concept established by Aristotle. You are accountable to the participants and your university for all your actions in the research process.

Reciprocity means that participants gain something from the research; there must be a quid pro quo (Corbin & Morse, 2003). They give you information, and in turn you lend them a listening ear, write their story, or make their voices heard and their concerns visible. Ethical rules also concern veracity and fidelity—truth telling and promise keeping. Truth telling means that you give participants and others involved in the research true information. You should also keep any promise you make to participants. Often doctoral students assure participants that they will receive feedback at the end of the study—if this is pledged, the promise must be kept. It might be possible to give a short summary of the research in writing to the participants as a thank you for the research information.

Ethics in Interviews and Observation

In informal and unstructured interviews, participants sometimes tend to disclose more than they wish but are not aware of having done so. Kvale and Brinkman (2009) state that the interview situation is sometimes seductive and intimate; because participants might regret disclosure later, ongoing consent is essential. Fear of disclosure of what they have said to their peers or senior staff is possible especially if they have criticized the organization and its management. Hence, keep the specific details confidential in order not to harm participants (or the institution).

Practical issues can also become problematic: indepth interviews can be very time consuming, and vulnerable people such as the sick, infirm elderly, and children might not be able to concentrate for long. In the case of such population groups, it would be better if you carried out shorter interviews and returned to participants later. Indeed, vulnerable people and individuals with learning difficulties need particular protection. For children and people with a mental disability, researchers are obliged to gain permission from parents or legal guardians, and ethical issues are complex. Not all members of these groups are able to give full informed consent, and some may not be able to read the information sheet or fill out the consent form. We would not advise using this type of sample for a doctoral study, given its time limitations, or when the researcher is inexperienced.

Always obtain permission to observe a situation or a setting; you need to reveal your presence and state the aim of the observation. There is only one case in which you need not declare your presence and ask for permission: in public places to which everybody has access—for instance, if you carry out observations at major sports events, or in street settings.

Covert observation is rarely permissible, and we would not advise it for doctoral students; for instance, covertly observing interactions between a tour guide and a group of tourists would not be appropriate, because this is a private situation. In public settings with unidentifiable clusters of people, it would be admissible—for example, observing groups of tourists at a heritage site could not be called unethical. In very specific circumstances and when it is essential to the research, however, covert observation might be possible. However, committees need good reasons to give permission for covert research.

Internet Research

Much research is now carried out via the Internet. Online interviews can generate problems with anonymity and confidentiality. Many participants believe that they are able to keep their anonymity by using a pseudonym, but we now know that online identities might accidentally be uncovered or deliberately sought by unscrupulous individuals; therefore, when reporting findings, you should create a pseudonym different from that used by your participant. (Another *caveat*: just going online these days, for any reason, can compromise your and others' privacy and identity; be careful of Internet use. The "cloud" is just a different name for other companies'/institutions' servers, and nothing is 100 percent secure on virtually any server.)

Ethics and Reflexivity

Ethics and reflexivity are closely linked concepts. Guillemin and Gillam (2004) ask researchers to adopt a reflexive stance throughout the planning and execution of the research not only as far as the generation of knowledge is concerned but also as a continuous process of "scrutiny and interpretation" (p. 275) and consideration of ethical dilemmas. (Misconduct, fabrication, and plagiarism in research are discussed in Chapter 9.)

Institutional Review Boards and Ethics Committees

As we have stated, obtaining approval for your research from the Ethics Committee and the Institutional Review Board of your university is an important step in your research. You should consult their guidelines and documents at an early stage. Review Boards are committees set up to judge research proposals and, on an ongoing basis, to scrutinize and monitor the ethics of the research. Universities in most countries have such committees (regardless of how they are labeled). They are in place to safeguard participants, the researcher, and the institution. Your proposal has to go to the relevant committee before you are allocated an advisory team. Only upon their agreement and with permission of your advisory team can you seek access to gatekeepers and start recruiting participants.

Ells (2011) recognizes the difficulty in persuading committees to accept and approve qualitative research, because of its flexible and dynamic character. We know of some doctoral students who deliberately change their proposals to include a structured interview schedule or a hypothesis rather than an interview guide in order to gain approval from the committee. According to Ells, however, these and other changes are detrimental to the study, because they damage the true spirit of qualitative research. Morse (2003) also acknowledges the difficulties in gaining approval for qualitative studies, partly because not all review boards have qualitative expertise. Morse and colleagues (2008) attribute difficulties in gaining permission to the emergent and unpredictable nature of qualitative research, with which review boards are often ill-equipped to deal. We believe, however, that things are improving. In many countries, the membership of ethics committees now includes specialists in qualitative research. You should adhere to the requirements of your institution. Ethical approval is always required, and you won't be able to publish without this.

We cannot discuss in this chapter every ethical dilemma that you might encounter, nor is there space to develop background notes to ethics and philosophy. If you are at all unsure of ethical issues or don't know how to solve ethical dilemmas, take guidance from your advisors. They will also know to which Institutional Review Board or Ethics Committee you should apply for approval.

Summary

- All researchers must consider ethical issues in research.
- The participant is entitled to confidentiality, anonymity, and privacy.
- Participation in the research is voluntary, and permission can be withdrawn.
- Qualitative research differs from quantitative research in the area of ethical issues.
- Fully informed consent is difficult to obtain because of the evolving, flexible nature of qualitative research.
- Permission to quote the participants in the dissertation or in publications needs to be obtained.
- Institutional Review Boards and Research Ethics Committees might not always understand the nature of ethics in qualitative research.

QUESTIONS AND ANSWERS

Question: *I wish to observe how physiotherapists interact with patients. My focus is on professional behavior. Do I need to disclose my presence not only to the health professionals but also to their clients?*

Answer: Yes, you do, although to put clients at their ease, you might explain that the purpose of your presence is to observe the physiotherapist.

Question: *My research requires access to vulnerable participants; what if I don't get access?*

Answer: You will not be able to do the research. Seek a different research question at an early stage; you might identify a similar topic with a different sample for which permission would be available.

Question: *My interviews might distress my participants. What should I do?*

Answer: You should have procedures in place, particularly if you interview vulnerable people. You might ask how they are feeling after the interview, or you might think it appropriate to refer them to a professional for counseling.

Question: *Do I really have to get permission from an Ethics Review Board? I've asked for volunteers through an advertisement in a newspaper, and my research does not deal with a sensitive topic. The participants in my study are mature adults and do not belong to a vulnerable group.*

Answer: You *always* need permission from your university to interview and observe people for doctoral research. But if your research topic isn't sensitive, and if your sample isn't vulnerable, you will probably find that permission is readily forthcoming.

Question: *I am having trouble recruiting participants and need to change the recruitment strategy. Do I need to return to the Ethics Review Panel?*

Answer: Yes, you do.

6. Role and Location of the Literature

Before you start your research you need to undertake an overview of the literature relevant to your study, because this activity defines and refines your topic and research question. Knowledge of the basic literature in the field is not only useful but also necessary for you to be able to show your background reading and to establish what you will contribute to the research. Also, some familiarity with the methodology and methods literature is essential at this stage. Resources for the literature review include

- textbooks at an appropriate level, including monographs and handbooks;
- scholarly, peer-reviewed journals;
- conference papers (sometimes published on the Internet or collated in readers).

You can also find material on journal databases and citation indices, as well as in previous dissertations and theses. An *Index of Theses* exists in Britain, and in the United States you can find *Dissertation Abstracts International*. Other countries have their own dissertation collections. Holland (2007) states that it is necessary not only to identify the key publications in the field but also to understand the broader context; even encyclopedias and glossaries of terms can be helpful. For searches in indices and databases you need appropriate key words. In our experience, one learns how to use the relevant search techniques through practice.

Essentials of a Qualitative Doctorate by Immy Holloway and Lorraine Brown, 69–78

Place of the Literature in Qualitative Inquiry

Qualitative and quantitative literature reviews differ considerably. Quantitative researchers generally carry out an extensive literature review related to their topic, whereas a different type of review is expected in qualitative research, which starts with an initial literature review and then integrates the literature into the findings and discussion.

Don't forget that the initial literature review and the proposal are not the start of the doctoral path but develop only after hard work and much critical thought and reflection on the research area and topic.

Initial Literature Review

The role and the function of the literature review at the start of your research are to

- establish the state of knowledge and theoretical positions in your field;
- identify gaps and show how your research will contribute to existing knowledge;
- define and refine the chosen topic and research question;
- assist in shaping the research question and arguments for your research;
- show how others inform your study and acknowledge their work;
- support the choice of approach taken;
- contextualize the research.

(See also Chenail, Cooper, & Desir, 2010; Daymon & Holloway, 2010; Ridley, 2008.)

Experts and inexperienced researchers differ in their views on the discussion of the literature at the start of a study. Some, for instance, propose that only foundational research should be discussed and little literature from previous studies should be presented, whereas others believe in a more thorough exploration of the literature at the very beginning.

We suggest a compromise: do not undertake an exhaustive literature review straight away but start with an initial overview of the landmark studies and pivotal research in your area of interest. Identify key authors in your field and show how your research might relate to their writing. Then discuss the major work related to the area of your study and enough literature to support your proposal, and establish an argument for carrying out your research.

- If you decide to carry out ethnographic research, for instance, a specific culture or subculture is the phenomenon under study. You might examine the concept of *culture* and the various ways in which it has been discussed by ethnographers in general and in your own field. Landmark studies of culture that are relevant for your research could also be examined.
- You know that interaction is an important issue in many grounded theory studies. You could discuss *interaction* and *symbolic interactionism* as central points in your literature review, as well as relevant studies that have been carried out in this arena. If you are a psychologist, the wider area of communication might also be important.

Many concepts or conceptual areas will be relevant for your study; because you need to be aware of their significance before your data collection and analysis start, you can discuss them without developing an exhaustive and indepth literature review from the very beginning. The research findings from other studies, however, should not direct you to a particular route or create bias before your work starts; this is the reason for not carrying out a fully comprehensive review. What you need is an overview of the literature in your area of study without being chained to specific ideas and directions. If you come across key concepts during your initial review, keep them in mind and note them for a later stage. Keeping abstracts also helps to inform a dialogue with the literature: this takes place once primary data have been collected and analyzed.

Nevertheless, you will have to give evidence from research that demonstrates whether, and how, other researchers have previously addressed the area and topic of your study, since you would not wish to duplicate another person's work. Morse (2003) suggests a broad approach to the literature in the planning phase and a presentation of a "theoretical/conceptual analysis" (p. 840), including a critical stance to previous work.

A doctoral student wishes to explore the general area of interaction between managers and employees. To help her to think about this, she examines theories of interaction and reads empirical studies of interaction in her own and other disciplines. This approach helps to focus her mind and allows her to identify a gap in knowledge.

You can see that the literature review at the start of the research has to be longer than just a few pages, which some students think sufficient, because it helps to define the boundaries of your literature review and to identify what you will include or exclude and where you will fill the gap in knowledge. However, variation is possible in the approach to the literature review, which is often influenced by the guidance of advisors and the chosen approach:

> Curtin (2008) did a comprehensive literature review before collecting primary data for her ethnographic study of wildlife tourism; Lugosi (2009) had only a brief introduction to his topic before presenting his primary findings on interaction in a gay bar; Shipway (2010) included an overview of the key areas in the introductory chapter to his doctoral dissertation on long-distance running.

Sometimes students may become confused over the role and location of the literature. For this reason, we advise that you discuss the subject in depth with your advisor.

> James read about the grounded theory approach and believed that there was no need for an initial literature review because he (mis)understood from his reading that it was not required at the start. His advisor strongly advised him, however, to compose an overview of the relevant research, because otherwise he would have no idea of what had been done in the field and might reinvent the wheel. He was also told that some of the literature was needed to formulate a coherent argument and rationale for his research.

As we have stated, some familiarity with the literature is desirable. An initial literature review shows what is out there, and how it relates to your study. It may be that the existing research poses a dissimilar research question, takes place in another country, or uses a different approach (or, indeed, may be full of flaws). Simply, your research should illuminate the topic from a different angle and employ a new perspective; as we have mentioned, attempt to persuade the reader that your research can make a valuable contribution to the field of study. (Many of the points made for the proposal also hold for the dissertation itself.)

To formulate a coherent argument for their research, researchers critically evaluate and assess what has already been done in the field. You might ask these questions:

1. Are the authors who have created this piece of writing credible and trustworthy?
2. Are their arguments convincing, and are the findings supported by evidence?
3. Does this writing present an early key study, or is it a recent important text?
4. Is the article or book relevant for your intended readership?
5. How would you do the study differently?

The authors' arguments are important, and so are their references. Have you read other material that originates from them, and have the authors a good reputation? Although the latter does not necessarily indicate flawless writing or good work, it helps to locate the writers in the area of study.

Richards and Morse (2007:221) give important advice to their students for the literature; we paraphrase some of their suggestions here. Researchers should examine

- how other writers provide evidence for the claims they make;
- how the evidence convinces the reader;
- how these writers gain the interest of their readers;
- how persuasive the arguments are;
- how these authors relate the literature to the findings;
- what does not seem right or appropriate for the study;
- how the researcher could have solved these problems.

If you follow these suggestions, your literature review will be appropriate.

You will undoubtedly have been reading on your topic area for a long while, and, of course, you cannot undo reading and reflection. Fetterman (2010:1), however, proposes that researchers begin "with an open mind, not an empty head." You must show that you have at least an overview and theoretical understanding of the area you wish to study. For this, a critical stance is needed to both content and method; do not provide merely a short summary of the research under discussion. This approach also helps to advance the formulation of the research question and to identify the gap in knowledge.

It is very rare that no, or very little, previous research has been done on the topic. The lack of any relevant literature makes the review difficult but does demonstrate the need for contribution to an important topic. If too much material exists in your area of inquiry, there is no point in doing qualitative research, because you would not be verifying or testing established hypotheses, and you do not wish to add to an already exhausted field of research. If you believe that no literature exists in the topic area, this might mean that your initial focus has been too restrictive and you have not embraced the larger field or examined studies in disciplines other than your own.

> A student undertaking a study of sustainable tourism in Kuwait found little relevant literature on business development in Islamic destinations in the tourism literature and had to venture outside her field of tourism to the discipline of anthropology.

In the initial review, the methodological literature also needs quoting and discussing. Consider these questions:

- Who are the early and influential writers who developed the approach you are using?
- In the field of methodology and method, what is the up-to-date and critical literature on this approach?
- How much use has been made of the approach in your discipline?

Answering these questions will help to justify your choice of approach at the proposal stage.

Ongoing Dialogue with the Literature

The bulk of the literature in qualitative research is tied to the themes that are generated by analysis. Research directly related to your findings is critically reviewed as the study proceeds. A dialogue of the relevant research with your own results takes place throughout the findings and/or discussion chapter.

The literature at this later stage has these functions:

- to integrate the existing research literature;
- to compare your findings with those of others;
- to examine whether the research literature confirms or challenges your own findings;
- to present an ongoing conversation with the research of others and to critically discuss the latter in light of your own research;
- to locate your research within the context of others' studies;
- to identify an original contribution.

As soon as you start analyzing your data, look at the relevant literature related to your study. Then compare the findings of the literature with your own findings. Sometimes the literature confirms your own findings; occasionally it contradicts (disconfirms) or challenges them. You can then develop a debate in which you set arguments about the differences or similarities, or give possible reasons why the literature confirms or challenges your own findings. It is also possible to illuminate and interpret others' research in the light of your own.

Some students make the mistake of perusing only the research in their specific field. You should broaden your search and examine studies that are directly relevant to the themes or categories that you discover, although they were not carried out in your particular discipline. As Richards and Morse (2007:192) suggest: "Knowledge fits incrementally, or by processes of replacement."

- A student carried out her research with new managers in business organizations. During her ongoing literature review she found research that had been done with nurses and educationalists. These studies related to her own emergent categories and could be debated and integrated with her findings even though the studies were located outside the management discipline.
- In research with lecturers in higher education, I. H. came across the *in vivo* code "thrown in at the deep end." She could compare this code with other studies where new professionals were also floundering, because they had no experience and had not been trained to deal with particular situations.
- In a discussion of "finding a new identity," a category related to long-distance running, Shipway (2010) collected studies on other sports in which sportsmen and -women searched for their identity.
- In a doctoral study of international student adjustment, food habits emerged as a major research category, necessitating the researcher (L. B.) to review the relevant anthropology literature, because so little research had been conducted on international student eating habits.

At the end of their initial discussion of the literature and beyond, researchers generally scan the literature again to add relevant new material that might interact with their findings. Don't neglect the latest research studies in your field, about which you might be asked in your examination. Although your conclusions should generally be drawn from your own data in relation to the aim of the research, it is appropriate to show where your own work is located within existing research.

Practical Issues

As an ongoing task, maintain a detailed list of all material relating to your research. We know from bitter experience that one sometimes forgets details; if you cannot find a particular article or book, or if you have run out of the time needed to find it, you will have to delete an important reference. To be well organized, you could distinguish between theoretical and empirical literature, the general and the specific, the subject-related and that linked to methods and methodology.

It is essential to read other qualitative dissertations to get an idea of how they should be formulated, but don't do this too early; otherwise, you might use them as a template for your own research, which is not advisable. We hope you have acquired library and search skills during your undergraduate or Masters years; if not, your library will update you, and your advisors will also help. Your advisors should in any case guide you toward the relevant literature, both in the area of method and that of content.

Summary

- The initial literature review is a critical examination of important studies related to the research area.
- The researcher identifies gaps in knowledge.
- The ongoing literature search relates to the researcher's findings.
- Researchers have a dialogue with the literature that confirms or challenges their own findings.
- The literature will be integrated and related to the work of the researcher.

QUESTIONS AND ANSWERS

Question: *I want to study this phenomenon because it is of great interest to me even though I know that it has been covered many times before. What shall I do?*

Answer: If there is too much literature and research on the topic you have chosen, find your own niche or a different angle, or choose another topic.

Question: *I have conducted an initial literature review on my topic and have found that nothing has been done on it. How can I proceed without a sound theoretical basis or a firm conceptual framework?*

Answer: An existing theoretical or conceptual framework is not necessary, because qualitative research does not start with deduction but is initially and mainly inductive. The framework develops during the research; however, theoretical ideas can be integrated from the beginning. Often—in grounded theory, for instance—you develop your own theory in the course of your study. Furthermore, you can look to related literature outside your own discipline, which will shed light on your topic.

Question: *My advisors require me to write an exhaustive literature review rather than an overview. What do I do?*

Answer: You might explain (diplomatically) that it is not laziness that prevents you from doing the exhaustive review but that you do not wish to be directed by the literature. Present them with an article or two that show you have followed expert advice in the way you have located the literature.

Question: *What if they still insist?*

Answer: It's not the end of the world. We have come across academics who insist on this rather deductive approach to qualitative research. Even if you include an exhaustive literature review, as some students are pressured into doing, you can still have a dialogue with the literature at the main findings stage.

Question: *What if my supervisors want a theoretical framework before the study?*

Answer: Tell them that you will develop theoretical perspectives during the research process. If they insist on the inclusion of a theoretical framework, make sure that you state that it may evolve during the course of the study.

Question: *I am nervous that my examiners might frown on a short literature review and that I might be penalized. Is there anything I can do to prepare for this?*

Answer: You could write in your methods chapter about the inductive nature of qualitative research and how it requires you to cover much of the literature after the data have been collected. This justifies your approach.

Question: *Any tips on organizing all the material, so that I don't lose important references and can find specific texts when I need them?*

Answer: Develop an alphabetical filing system on your computer with the exact reference information and a short summary and anything interesting that you have noted. Update it regularly, back it up, and make a printout, so you won't lose it.

The Research Journey

7. The Monitoring Process

dvisors, supervisors, and mentors are those who oversee and counsel
you on your doctoral study, be it in the topic area or in the research
methodology and methods; here we use the term *advisor*. This chapter addresses the issues that arise in most doctoral advisory relationships,
although in qualitative research you may experience more problems than
those faced by students doing quantitative research, owing to misun-
derstandings of the unique procedures associated with using qualitative
methods.

The right advisor is a crucial element in the completion and success
of your doctorate. You should remember, however, that members of the
advisory team are not meant to do the work for you. We have come across
instances when students forget this; they expect advisors not only to support and counsel but also to do some of the work for them, although this
happens mainly in the early stages.

> *At the beginning of the relation-
> ship with your advisors, negotiate
> ground rules for collaboration.*

Role and Responsibilities of Advisors and Students

An early stage in the process of writing a doctoral study involves choosing
an advisor. You might already know a variety of academics in your faculty
who work in your field and even some who are experts in your specific

Essentials of a Qualitative Doctorate by Immy Holloway and Lorraine Brown, 81–90
© 2012 Left Coast Press, Inc. All rights reserved.

area of study. Obviously it would be better to choose these people as advisors rather than somebody who has only a vague knowledge of your topic. Of course, it is possible that an advisor might be *au fait* with the specific research approach you intend to adopt. In any case, it's a good idea to include an expert.

Look up the potential advisors' records of publication, ask other students who have completed or are in the process of undertaking a doctoral dissertation their opinion on these potential advisors. Gain their view on the academics' style of work and interaction with their students, because it is critical that you be able to get on with your advisors. Some have a formal approach to their work with students; others adopt an informal stance to interaction. Choose advisors whose style of work you like, always keeping in mind the importance of their expert knowledge. Your faculty might have only a few who have the right qualities for *you*. You might, however, not get the chance to choose your own advisors within a department; they might be assigned—practice and resources vary from institution to institution.

Responsibilities of Doctoral Advisors

Doctoral advisors have many responsibilities; they are accountable to students and the university, and they have their own research reputation and career to uphold. Often they also tutor undergraduates. Holloway and Walker (2000:39) suggest that advisors

- help their students to get to know the university, the department, and their peers;
- make sure that the students get the appropriate research training;
- advise and mentor students;
- give appropriate and frequent feedback to students;
- see that students follow ethical guidelines;
- support students throughout their research journey;
- write progress reports and fill out relevant official papers;
- where they lack knowledge, find appropriate experts whom students can contact;
- assist in publishing papers.

One of the most important factors in the interaction of student and advisors is feedback. Advisors give feedback in three ways: orally, in writing, and by email (Li & Seale, 2007a). As long as there is frequent, reasonably prompt and constructive feedback, you will have a good chance of success in your doctoral journey.

Student Responsibilities

Students should

- negotiate a program of study and meetings with their advisors;
- set up a system of regular meetings, depending on whether they are full- or part-time;
- keep advisors informed of all developments or changes during the research process;
- write regular progress reports whenever required to do so (for advisors and the research degree committee);
- submit written work, if required, in advance of meetings;
- discuss academic and/or practical problems;
- inform advisors of personal problems if they impinge on the research process and progress;
- behave in an ethical manner.

In general, advisors hope that students take their advice, especially if the latter have little experience in serious research. You need a good reason not to follow the advice given to you, although in the end, of course, you are the person who is responsible for your study. You have to justify your course of action in both the dissertation and in the oral defense. Saying "because my advisor told me to" is never an acceptable explanation for what you have done.

> As the research proceeds, you become more and more independent. YOU will be the expert in your area of study when you have completed the research.

At the start of the research, you might expect more advice and guidance, but your advisors will expect you to become more independent as you grow to be more confident and knowledgeable. Toward the very end of your study, they might feel that you need more support and counsel again, because this stage is critical. Of course, feedback should be given on all draft chapters that you submit to your advisors.

Problems in the Relationship with Your Advisors

During the research process you might experience problems with your advisors, especially in the very beginning when you don't know each other well. One problem might be to do with the style of your advisors, which might not suit you. You need to resolve this problem very quickly; otherwise, your doctoral process will be hindered. Initially, at least, you have the responsibility to try hard to adapt to your advisors' ways and to understand them (in the hope that they will do the same). If, after much effort at understanding from both sides, advisors' acting and thinking are really different from yours, try to change advisors quickly—but, of course, this is not always possible.

- Luis, an extrovert, optimistic, and cheerful person, found at an early stage in the doctoral process that his main advisor was very earnest and ritualistic, and so he found it difficult to relate. Also, John thought his advisor took an inappropriate stance both to him and his topic, which involved the marketing field. However, after a while, and a number of meetings, John found to his surprise that he started to like his advisor, who always had time for him. He also found that his advisor had a dry sense of humor. Over time, the two developed a good relationship.
- Jennifer had an advisor who always joked around and never took her study seriously. Although Jennifer tried hard to get on with her advisor, she found her jokes offensive and rude, and she felt that she could not work with this person. She asked for another advisor by telling the Head of Research that the advisory style did not suit her at all. The Head of Research told Jennifer to try getting on with her advisor, because there were not many people available who could be on the team. After some discussions, however, her advisor was changed.

Do make an attempt to adapt to your advisors; ultimately you may have to work with them.

Academic Problems in Interaction with Advisors

The academic issues that you might have to deal with in the advisory or supervision process are these:

1. You cannot easily gain access to your advisors, and they have little time for you.
2. Your advisors don't give you enough guidance and are not critical.
3. Your advisors give too much direction and advice.

4. Your advisors lack expertise or knowledge in the area of study or the methodology you wish to adopt.
5. Members of the advisory team give you conflicting advice.
6. One or several or your advisors leave, and you are allocated to new staff.

1. Nonresponse of Advisors   This problem is probably the most common complaint among doctoral students. Academics, of course, are busy people, and they cannot always give you time at the moment you need it. You can solve this problem (usually) by setting up a series of initial meetings over a time span and after this by negotiating a future date for your meeting each time you see your advisors. Exchange email addresses and telephone numbers; some advisors even give their home phone numbers to their students, especially if they have arrived at a crucial stage in the study. You can improve your relationship with advisors by informing them of meeting cancellations well in advance, but don't cancel unless it is absolutely necessary—because of illness, bereavement, or serious family problems, for instance.

You might expect the same consideration from your advisors. If an advisor is nonresponsive even after several attempts from you at contact, inform the research administrator, head of research, or even the head of department or faculty. It is your right to have contact with and feedback from your advisors, given the crucial role they play in the research process. However, we know from experience that students are hesitant to complain for fear of censure and of disrupting the relationship with the advisor; this is particularly true of students from a culture high in power distance. If you are tactful about this situation, however, no retribution will come from reporting nonresponse; what will happen initially is that the administrator will get in touch with the advisors and ask them to initiate contact with you.

Aiko sent draft copies of her chapter to her advisors and heard nothing back from them for two months, even though she had sent them several emails asking to meet them for feedback. In frustration, she went to see another academic in the department, who reported the situation to the research degree administrator. Through Aiko's diplomatic negotiation and the administrator's tactful talk with the advisors, the situation was soon resolved. Even though Aiko was nervous about registering a complaint, she knew that she had no choice, as it was impossible to complete without advice.

2. Inadequate Feedback   A second common complaint concerns inadequate feedback on written work: for example, an advisor might read the work you sent just before the meeting and make only a few minor comments on it. Advisors are supposed to be "critical friends," and receiving constructive criticism is an essential part of being a doctoral student. If there is no critical feedback, you might not succeed.

> Daniel had two advisors, one who gave him regular and detailed feedback and one who rarely commented on his work, even though he was the person with subject expertise. After a number of months, Daniel delicately raised this problem with the first advisor, who promised to intercede on his behalf. From then on, the feedback from both advisors was prompt and, of course, useful.

Unfortunately, advisors are sometimes negligent, and you might never manage to "educate" the one who does not respond or send feedback. If nothing gets changed in spite of your best efforts, either set up a complaints procedure or work independently and find somebody else in the faculty to become your unofficial advisor.

3. Guidance versus Control   A third problem concerns the thin boundary between guidance and control. Guidance is necessary; control is inappropriate. At a relatively early stage you should have some autonomy in your research. Gently and firmly, at a stage when you have become knowledgeable in both topic and method, show your advisors that you expect some independence in doing your research and that you do not need excessive direction.

The British authors Phillips and Pugh, in *How to Get a PhD* (2010), devote one chapter to "How to Manage Your Supervisor." Managing—and educating—your advisors are diplomatic skills that you need to learn. If you feel that your advisory team wishes you to change your topic or research question, think hard about it. Do they have good reasons for you to go in a different direction?

> Annabel worried that an advisor was pushing her in the direction of a theoretical framework that she didn't care for—first, because it was an angle on the research that she didn't want to prioritize and, second,

because it undermined the inductive approach that she wanted to adopt. Because this advisor wasn't trained in and knowledgeable about qualitative research, it was hard for Annabel to convince him that such a framework wasn't necessary. She could only "stand up to" this advisor with the help of another person on the advisory team.

The issue of advisory criticism should also be kept in mind. It is great if you have advisors who will criticize you as well as guide and support you. Some individuals are more direct than others and tell you straight; others are more sensitive in their comments. Some advisors prefer that the student hears their critique clearly rather than having to search for cues in the feedback. (Li and Seale [2007a] suggest that there are four types of criticism: *direct* and *indirect* criticism, criticism with *caution,* and criticism with *guidance* and *support*.)

> *Don't be offended by criticism.*
> *To be critical—in a constructive*
> *way—is the task of an advisor.*

4. Advisors' Lack of Expertise   Often advisors have differing levels of expertise; some might be more knowledgeable in the field of the research topic, others in the methodology and methods. Most universities, except for some small institutions, have experts in your topic area—otherwise, you would not have chosen to study at your institution. In any case, for a doctoral study you will quickly become well read in your topic area and acquire some expertise yourself; and you may surpass the expertise of your advisor. For methodology and methods, however, you need at least one specialist on your team who has expertise in your area.

Geerd felt unfortunate that neither of his advisors had subject expertise in his chosen area; it had been impossible for his department to find advisors with expert knowledge of the topic. Thus his advisors acted as mentors and as educated readers of his work, but he was basically cast adrift and left to search the literature unaided. This situation did not detrimentally affect his progress, however: he successfully completed his doctorate within the allocated timeframe. What both advisors could offer was extensive experience and advice on the qualitative *method* he had adopted, and they asked an academic from a different university to give some help to the student if consulted.

This is not an ideal situation; it is possible that this candidate coped well because he was an academic colleague, with years of experience and familiarity with the relevant literature.

5. Conflicting Advice   Members of your advisory team will sometimes have different opinions and offer conflicting advice. This can lead to fruitful debates about the area of disagreement, which can be entertaining and useful for students. However, such debate can sometimes be unnerving when differing advice takes students in different directions, and it is of little comfort to be told "it is your research, it is your decision."

- Rachel was advised by one of her advisors experienced in qualitative methods that she should integrate findings and discussion. This kind of integration is often a distinguishing feature of qualitative research; however, her other advisor was not comfortable with it. He advised that results and discussion should be separated, as is common in the reporting of quantitative research. Rachel was discomfited by this display of disagreement and conflict and was nervous about following the advice of the qualitative expert, who was the junior member of the team in respect of seniority in the department.
- Greta carried out phenomenological research and wished to integrate findings and discussion. Her first advisor was a phenomenologist, thus she was persuaded to write separate chapters on findings and discussion. This is often done in phenomenology, although it is not a strict rule for this approach.

6. Change of Advisors   If an advisor or a supervisor leaves your academic institution, which happens frequently, the doctoral or research committee will search for a person with expertise in your field and/or your research approach. It occasionally happens, if the university allows, that the person who has left will remain part of the team. In any case, your university has the responsibility to recruit appropriate advisors for your team.

Summary

- The advisory team should have knowledge of the chosen area of research and the research methodology.
- Students and advisors maintain regular contact throughout the research process.
- Written work is presented by students to their advisors in their meetings.
- Students can expect regular feedback on their writing.

QUESTIONS AND ANSWERS

Question: *My advisor wants me to manage my research her way, but I wish to go in a different direction. What do I do? Do I have to do as she says?*

Answer: Do think carefully about this; the advice may be sound and save you many problems at a later stage. Remember that your advisor is experienced and is aware of the pitfalls you may face. However, if you feel very strongly, try to persuade her to your point of view. This means that you and she will still be able to work together.

Question: *How do I know what advice to take from my advisors and when to disagree with their advice?*

Answer: Initially you will probably follow all advice given. When you become more confident in your area of work, when you become knowledgeable about the literature in the field, you might have discussions with your advisors and sometimes reject their counsel.

Question: *Is it useful to meet with other doctoral students to share experiences and to form action learning groups?*

Answer: Yes, this is very good practice, because just knowing that you are not alone in the problems you face can relieve stress, and you can help one another to solve the problems you encounter during the research.

Question: *One of my advisors is remiss in terms of feedback, and yet I have been advised that I should include her name on papers that I write. I don't want to do this, because I don't feel she has contributed to my study—although I am happy to co-author with the advisor who did contribute.*

Answer: It is often politically advisable to put your advisors' names on your paper, especially if you want a career in academia, but this is your choice. If said advisor has not contributed to the paper or the dissertation, it is your right to exclude him or her as an author.

Question: *I have two advisors: one who is a senior academic (a professor) and one who is a junior member of staff, who is, however, an expert in qualitative research. There is often conflict between the two on how to approach my study, and I often find that I want to heed the advice given by the junior academic—but I fear censure from the professor. What should I do?*

Answer: This is a difficult position for you; however, you should not be nervous about reprisals from one advisor if you choose to listen to advice from the other. Make sure that you weigh the guidance given by both and follow the advice that means most to you, especially if it is supported by the qualitative research texts. Making and standing by such decisions is an important aspect of the doctoral journey.

Question: *I definitely wish to change my advisor for various reasons. What shall I do?*

Answer: Such change is a delicate and diplomatic process. Think about it carefully. First look at the institutional guidelines about advisors. Talk about it with the relevant member of staff, head of research, or head of faculty who can give you advice. Be mindful of sensitivities when discussing it with anybody.

8. The Qualitative Research Process

Throughout this book, you will have detected a sequence for conducting doctoral research. However, we do not wish to convey the idea that this course is straightforward or chronological, or that it progresses in even steps. It is instead iterative, meaning that it goes back and forth, as you continuously revisit the research question, the data, the analysis, and the findings. Reflexivity is the built-in reflection process that helps you to reexamine your assumptions and those of your participants.

By its very nature the doctoral journey is a process of inquiry that answers specific questions and illuminates an important issue or phenomenon. Do keep in mind the following quality criteria for a doctoral dissertation (Holloway & Walker, 2000):

- a contribution to knowledge in the field of study;
- originality, uniqueness, and creativity;
- independent, critical, and analytic thinking;
- coherence.

Starting to Write

Most advisors counsel students to start writing from the very beginning of the research and to make writing an ongoing process. Your advisors are obliged to provide you with regular feedback throughout the doctoral process, as we described earlier. As we also mentioned, feedback is a key issue

Essentials of a Qualitative Doctorate by Immy Holloway and Lorraine Brown, 91–103

in qualitative research, particularly at the beginning of your work when you need to find your way. It is also important toward the end, when you have to consider explanations for and interpretations of your findings. Qualitative inquiry includes many ambiguities with which you will have to cope. Regular writing will help you to refine your thinking.

If you have written a detailed proposal, you can use some of it in your dissertation. For instance, the rationale for your research, its setting and context, will stay the same, as will your methodology section, but, at a later stage, you should add detailed examples from the study itself. Of course, you won't prepare your final introduction before you complete your research.

Go to your advisory meetings with some written material: perhaps a methodology section, or a discussion of a category you have generated from analysis. It's also a good idea to take a list of questions that you would like to ask your advisors.

When presenting findings writers usually include quotes from their participants to show that the themes, categories, or descriptions are grounded in the data. These quotes should come from a variety of participants rather than just a few. Bear in mind the qualitative approach to writing up findings: you should be prepared to interpret your findings and bring in the relevant literature.

Organizing the Dissertation

At the very beginning, create an outline or similar structure for your study. At certain stages of your work you can revisit this outline and see whether or how you have diverged from it—don't worry, this is common; the research process demands flexibility. Your advisory team will be grateful to receive this outline, which will enable them to check your progress and diversions; indeed, you might take their advice about preparing it before you write it down. Structure this outline in detail, with headings and subheadings; this systematic approach will make the writing process much easier. (Of course, the outline is not written in stone; it can change as the dissertation progresses.)

A good filing index for articles related to the research topic and area of study will assist you in your writing. You may find articles/books during the research process, but at a later stage you will organize them by theme or priority. To safeguard your records and your work, be sure to back everything up, whether electronically or as hard copy (for example, by photocopying). This precaution applies to all aspects of the research, from the literature to raw primary data and analysis; and be sure to keep several copies in different locations. A colleague of ours lost all his material because of a fire in his building; he had kept his work and backed-up copies in one physical location. Another colleague took her work on holiday, and her briefcase with both hard and soft copies was stolen. A useful tip is to regularly email work to yourself, which can be accessed from anywhere in the world. Using a cloud-based back-up service is also a good precaution.

Keeping Records and Storing Thoughts

Record keeping and "storing ideas" (Richards & Morse, 2007) are important activities throughout the research process. Write or record all the ideas and theoretical reflections that arise during the research from the very beginning. Diaries, fieldnotes, and memos are the main forms for such records. In many dissertations, excerpts from these documents find their way into the findings chapters.

[*month/day/year*]

I soon realized that it was a distressing experience for international students to be interviewed about the shock they experienced on arrival in the new country; many students were in tears as they spoke of their loneliness and homesickness. I realized that I had to handle participants with care and resolved to follow up on them a few days after the interview had taken place.

(*This note found its way into the ethics section of the dissertation.*)

Your field diaries are written comments or reflections on your experience: you may make notes by hand, but type them up at a later date and on a regular basis so you can keep track of them. Also, treat such notes as data; thus you should date, label, and number them for easy access.

Memos are reports on the analytic process, and they can help later in the development of theories or descriptions. Strauss (1987) defined them as an internal dialogue going on throughout the research; Charmaz (2006) claims that memoing helps to develop ideas and to make comparisons and connections.

We advise you to record an insight or idea as soon as it comes to you; otherwise, it may be lost. It can be expanded at a later date.

> One of us did a great deal of research before writing up but took no notes, thinking "it is all there in my head." To her distress, she found during the writing stage that she had forgotten some of the ideas that had emerged in the early stages of her work. She now always reminds her students to start writing early, to make it an ongoing process, and to write regular notes.

A useful way to make the research task more manageable is to make notes every week or so about what you have achieved so far and what you will achieve in coming days, breaking the doctoral project into discrete tasks, into flexible guidelines.

Keep records such as fieldnotes, memos, and a research diary throughout your study—you will need these.

Producing Data

Before you start generating data, sort out your sampling and how to get access to the participants. Most students we know are quite clear about the people they wish to sample (although it is difficult to be precise at the beginning of a qualitative study), but they forget to tell the reader how they gained access to the people in the sample.

Once you have decided on your participants, you need to consider how to generate data. As we mentioned earlier, interviewing and observing people are the most common ways of produce data. Indepth, unstructured interviews are often the best way of collecting rich and deep data, but semi-structured interviews can also be appropriate. You will usually have some keywords to remind you how to develop the indepth interview, or an interview guide (not schedule) for semistructured interviews. As you proceed, you will become progressively more focused in that you might decide to concentrate on specific areas that advance your research and seem most important to you or the participants.

Interviews can be complemented by participant observation, and often by diaries and documents (although generally phenomenology and narrative inquiry do not include formal participant observation). Your decisions depend entirely on your research question and aim. Interviews and observation need reflection and preparation, although they should be flexible. By the way, don't forget that an interview question is not the same as a research question. We occasionally find that our students muddle these. Interview questions are steps toward answering the research question and are more specific.

If you are following an innovative approach in the performative social sciences, you might generate visual data, including photographs, paintings, and films. As you know, qualitative research often generates an overload of data, of which you need to make sense (see Chapter 9). The skills of management, analysis, and interpretation are vital to sorting through all these data.

Regular discussion of your analysis, reflections, and interpretations should be held with your advisors, which should be complemented by regular reflective writing and musings on the themes of your research.

Examining, Exploring, and Interpreting the Data

As you know, different approaches involve different ways of analyzing data; therefore, make sure that you revisit and familiarize yourself with the specific method of analysis associated with your approach. We focus here on shared issues among the approaches. Three main pitfalls to avoid are neglecting to ground your analysis in the data (we have often seen student work that fails to offer data in the form of quotations and fieldnotes that illustrate the analytic point being made); under-discussing your data; forgetting to engage in a dialogue with the related literature. A reflexive approach to writing will help you to avoid these pitfalls. Reflexivity, as you know, involves "critical self-scrutiny" (Etherington, 2004).

Concept Maps, Diagrams, and Flowcharts

A useful way to detect patterns and relationships in data is by mapping concepts in a graphic form (Daley, 2004). Developed in educational psychology, concept mapping is a graphic presentation and illustration of the major research ideas, and the relationships between them, that emerge from your data analysis. Although it is generally popular in quantitative inquiry, where it follows a prescribed path, it is used informally in all types of research. A concept map (which could be useful in any phase of your

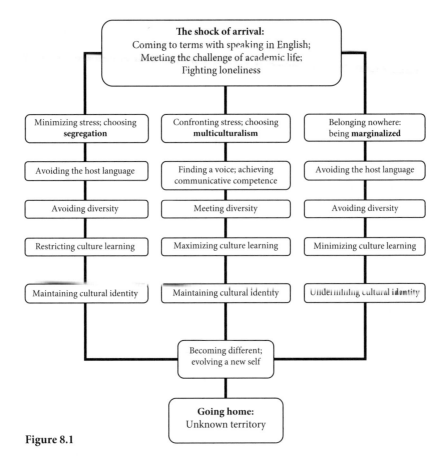

Figure 8.1

study) will help your thinking at the analysis stage. Such diagrams present a simplified picture of ideas and concepts and points to interrelationships in data. (See Figure 8.1 for an example of a pictorial depiction of the research categories generated by an ethnographic study of international student adjustment.)

Formulating an Argument

An argument is a reasoned statement backed by evidence that persuades others of a particular viewpoint or supports a conclusion about the data. It can be debated and refuted by contrary evidence or supported by confirming evidence. Doctoral students have to develop arguments to convince their readers that they have analyzed their data and reflected on them. This

96

approach helps to answer the crucial "so what?" question for which you need a response (Charmaz, 2006). You have to work at the formulation of arguments; they don't just emerge miraculously from the data. Charmaz (p. 157) advises students to complete these statements at regular junctions in the research:

My argument is . . .
My reasoning is . . .
I support this argument by including . . .

Initially arguments might be provisional, especially during the data-collection process, but they firm up during the course of the analysis. Indeed, ideas for arguments come directly from your data analysis. Beware of producing arguments that lack supporting evidence; and do not theorize beyond the data collected. Your arguments should usually be based on the evidence of a number of participants rather than just one or two. You need many examples (and quotes from different participants) from the data to sustain your arguments. Be sure to consider alternative explanations as well as contrary occurrences: this will make your argument stronger.

Mason (2002:176–177) describes different types of argument, which we have slightly modified:

- arguments that are based on evidence (I can make this argument because evidence for it exists);
- arguments that are interpretive or narrative (I shall demonstrate that I can interpret and give meaning to the data);
- arguments that are evocative or illustrative (I can show understanding and empathy for the participants and give an illustration for the argument);
- reflexive or multivocal arguments (I will show a multiplicity of perspectives and voices, including my own).

Arguments can be compared and contrasted with the literature; this will spur development of the study.

Interpretation

Interpretation in qualitative research is closely allied with analysis and means making sense of the data and findings, by conceptualizing or theorizing about them. No qualitative research is purely descriptive but relies on conceptualizing and theorizing, whereby you link the findings to the meaning that emerge from them. Speculation about the meaning and implications of the findings needs close links to the data and has to be grounded in evidence. It is appropriate that the emic and the etic perspective are shown separately, but the latter has its roots in the former. Keep in mind potential alternative interpretations and check them against the data. The statements you make should never go beyond the specific research findings and the reading connected to them. Do not be too sure of your interpretations; always search for possible alternatives. If the interpretation is well done, the reader should understand it.

> *During the research process you will take the important step of going from the data—the perceptions, experiences, and thoughts of the participants—to a level of abstraction and theorizing that is necessary to achieve doctoral standards.*

Problems in Analysis and Interpretation

Li and Seale (2007b:1445) point toward four types of problems linked to doctoral students' data analysis:

- not knowing where to begin;
- ambiguous coding;
- reporting and recording problems;
- inaccurate interpretation or over-interpretation.

Many of our students have experienced these problems in their analysis. Even with guidance, some candidates do not know where to start analyzing the data. Usually we advise to begin with small steps rather than trying to manage large amounts of material, to look at one interview (or observation) and analyze that. Li and Seale also suggest that students insert line numbers in their transcripts, a practice that makes it easier to report and record problems. Once students become more confident, they feel comfortable with the analysis process. Thorough knowledge of coding, categorizing, labeling, and other ways of analysis is necessary and relates to the chosen approach. Over-interpretation and inaccuracies occur when students find meanings that are not confirmed by the evidence from the data sources and when they invent or imagine them. (A discussion of problems follows in the next chapter.)

Role of Theory in Qualitative Research

Of course, qualitative research does not start out with developed theories, although it can be linked to them. New theoretical ideas develop during the research, and indeed GT produces a theory. Although themes and meanings come directly from the data, they do not emerge naturally and without effort. You have to work to extract the meanings and to develop theory.

Existing theory can also be interwoven and integrated from your disciplinary perspective. Even qualitative research is not purely inductive, and theory is always involved in knowledge development. Researchers theorize continuously when they generate and organize ideas. For instance, if you complete a piece of ethnographic research on tourist behavior, you might build in theoretical ideas about culture; and a grounded theory study on interaction that ostensibly develops theory will probably include ideas about symbolic interactionism. Even the choice of methodology involves theorizing, because it is based on the researcher's ideas about the nature of being and knowledge. Tavallaei and Atalib (2010) maintain that there is a clear link between methodologies and theories.

Validity or Trustworthiness

You need to check and report on the validity of your data and findings. Guba and Lincoln (1989), Strauss and Corbin (1998), and others use a variety of terms for qualitative research, such as *trustworthiness*, *authenticity*, and *credibility*, but the nomenclature is immaterial as long as you realize that validity criteria are different for qualitative and quantitative research. Some people would even suggest that validity criteria are irrelevant in qualitative research; indeed, there is no consensus on validity in the qualitative community, but readers and researchers would generally expect that you have some quality criteria and that you discuss these. The validity check is carried out through

- reflexivity;
- contextualization;
- "prolonged engagement" (Lincoln and Guba);
- thick description;

- audit trail;
- member checks,
- triangulation.

The first four of these concepts have been described in Chapter 1, but we need to give an explanation of the others. An *audit trail* refers to the description of research decisions that researchers make and document throughout the study. This trail can be followed by the reader of the research to assess its soundness.

Doing a *member check* means that researchers return their interpretations and conclusions to the individual participants in the study, who check whether they faithfully and adequately reflect the participants' social world. Many qualitative researchers feel ambivalent about this process, because once interpreted and theorized, the data offered by participants may be so transformed that they are unrecognizable to lay readers. Many researchers, particularly phenomenologists, see member checking as inappropriate (see Angen, 2000; Carlson, 2010; McConnell, Chapman, & Francis, 2011).

The term *triangulation* refers to the use of several research methods within one study. A mixed-methods approach would provide triangulation. However, many qualitative researchers do not use between-method triangulation but stay instead within method, meaning that they use different data sources, such as interviewing, observation, and documents *within* qualitative research methodology. (For a longer discussion see Denzin, 2009.)

Toward a Conclusion

The analysis and interpretation of the data lead directly to the conclusion to your research, which must be grounded in your findings; the data are your supporting evidence.

You need to revisit the research question and aim of your study and see whether you have achieved the latter (see Chapter 2). The conclusion rallies your arguments; it captures and presents the essence of your study. You need to show in the conclusion how you have contributed to knowledge in your field. Qualitative researchers are generally careful not make claims that go beyond their findings or beyond their specific setting, although they sometimes make theoretical gencralizations. Don't try to cram everything you have found out into the conclusion; include only that which advances your major arguments.

Telling a Story

The best way to convey your findings is by telling a story. Who are the main players, what are their thoughts and feelings, what is the plot? Your dissertation, the account of the research, is a narrative that must be coherent and engage the reader—although it is not necessarily chronological. All qualitative research approaches demand attention to writing style and try to stay faithful to the tales told by participants and the way they give meaning to their behavior. The final report, although being an academic piece of work that will be peppered with academic references and theorizing, should have coherence, readability, and the power to engage the audience.

Publishing during the Research Process

Institutions and advisors have different views on publishing articles during development of the research and writing of the thesis. Some maintain that it's better to complete the study first, because publication, which is time consuming, hinders the smooth progression of the dissertation. Other universities encourage their doctoral students to publish. There are several advantages to early publishing: It helps candidates to think clearly and to develop their reasoning and arguments, particularly if the feedback from reviewers is thorough and constructive, and it gets individuals used to writing coherently. Because the doctoral research process is long, a student might become demotivated, in need of new stimulation and impetus that writing an article could provide. It might also assist the future career of doctoral students, who could develop a small portfolio of articles at the start of their academic or professional life; mature students, who are already part of a profession, could enhance their reputation.

Furthermore, Oliver (2008:152) advocates publishing as "a useful exercise in academic writing," because it helps to develop succinct and sophisticated writing skills. Also, it is useful to pass a copy of your publications to the examination team, who will become aware of your hard work and standing in the academic community.

However, early publishing also carries drawbacks. Academic articles differ from doctoral dissertations; they are much shorter, and they demand a different style of writing. You could spend a lot of time writing when you should be developing your work (we would never advise a student who is lagging behind to publish articles). You might also struggle to find the appropriate journal in which to publish; this could also be time consuming.

In general, we believe that you should not publish during the research process if you are a first time researcher, if your time is very limited, or if you are struggling with your dissertation. We would, however, recommend publication to those doctoral students who wish to pursue an academic career, who are familiar with the publishing process, and who are confident about and up to date with their research.

Your advisors will probably suggest that you attend conferences during the research process. Regardless of the stage of your research, you will always be able to present a paper, even in the early phase; for example, you might discuss your initial literature review, methodological issues, and your experience of the research process. Feedback from conference delegates—be they doctoral students, experienced researchers, or experts in the field—will help you to advance your study. It will also give you a chance to practice presenting, explaining, and defending your research, which will be good preparation for the doctoral exam.

> - One of our students, who is exploring the experiences of people with inherited thrombophilia, presented an early paper on the social construction of the gene. Discussion with her peers and experts helped her to develop her ideas on her study.
> - Another student presented a paper on the transformative potential of tourism and learned from feedback that she should not talk in generalized terms and that she needed to specify that this potential was not realizable by all segments of the tourist population.

Our next chapter will be about presenting the findings and writing the research report.

Summary

- Doctoral students need to organize and manage their data.
- During the research process students should keep writing so that they are not overwhelmed at the end of the data-collection and analysis process.
- Fieldnotes, diaries, and memos is important memory aides, and they help in the development of ideas.
- Formulating academic arguments is a necessary part of the dissertation development process.
- Going to conferences and receiving feedback help students to develop ideas.

QUESTIONS AND ANSWERS

Question: *When should I start writing?*

Answer: Start as soon as you have something to write about. Show some of the writing to your advisor, because you work more productively when you have feedback.

Question: *Should I do semistructured or unstructured interviews?*

Answer: That depends on what and how you intend to research. In narrative research, unstructured interviews might be better, because they allow an uninterrupted flow of participants' ideas. In GT, semistructured interviews are more appropriate, because the research is more focused from the beginning. There is no hard rule for most approaches.

Question: *I'm basing my study on interviews and observations. How many of each of these should I do?*

Answer: There is no set number of interviews. Go on until you find nothing new or important for your agenda. The same is appropriate for observations, but take care that you are immersed in the setting for some time.

Question: *My interview style has improved with practice, and later interviews were much richer. Should I discount early data?*

Answer: No, you will find useful ideas in the early data, too.

Question: *I have been advised to separate my findings from my discussion. I find this very difficult, because I am generating much repetition, and the account might lack coherence. Can I go against this advice and integrate findings and discussion?*

Answer: Qualitative research is flexible. If you do this integration well, it is appropriate to integrate findings and discussion.

9. Problems in the Research Process

Everybody who carries out research encounters problems during the process, and you will be no exception. It is best to tackle problems as they arise and not wait until near the completion of the research, when you might get into a panic. Don't forget that advisers are there to support you; other faculty members who have knowledge on the method or topic might also be able to help. Problems can usually be divided into two main groups: academic difficulties and personal issues. These are not always completely separate; they often overlap.

Academic Problems

Academic problems include

1. anxiety or lack of confidence;
2. drowning in data, or lack of data;
3. writer's block;
4. duplication of the research;
5. organization and time management;
6. lack of focus.

1. Anxiety or Lack of Confidence

Lack of confidence is a real stumbling block to completion. At some stage, usually early in your study, you might experience a lack of confidence in

Essentials of a Qualitative Doctorate by Immy Holloway and Lorraine Brown, 105–115

yourself, especially if your advisors are severe and penetrating in their critique of your work. Try not to take critique personally: it is the advisors' duty to criticize (constructively) so that your study improves. Students are often too close to their research to spot errors and areas that need work. One student told us that she dreaded sending work to supervisors because of the debilitating, although constructive, feedback she received in reply. Your acceptance as a doctoral student indicates that the university is confident that you will be able to complete the work. Doing academic work, whether a doctorate or a journal article, involves peer review and a consequent opening of yourself to judgment, and you need to develop a thick skin. The more you expose yourself to peer critique, the easier the process becomes.

Maria acknowledged

... a constant worry of not being "clever" enough. There is always more to learn, and I think this is a confidence issue both when talking to other lecturers and to fellow students.

Lack of confidence often generates anxiety. Owler (2010:298) states that candidates often experience "an intense oscillation between excitement and anxiety in the doctoral process." You might feel particularly anxious at the very beginning of your research. We know of colleagues who lost sleep over the momentous decision to start their doctoral journey: this was caused by anxiety over workload and over their perceived inability to succeed.

In the first year you will probably feel very enthusiastic and want to forge ahead. Thinking about the potential data collection seems to provide impetus and motivation for most students. However, your advisers might suggest that much work needs to be carried out—especially reading about your methodology—before you can really start on your data collection. This pressure will frustrate you and make you anxious, because you will be eager to start the data collection promptly. Read about your approach and try not to become impatient. Knowledge of method will help during the process of the research; indeed, with some approaches you could go seriously wrong if you start collecting data without knowledge of approach and procedures.

> In a rush to meet a deadline, one of our doctoral students started to collect data before her method had been properly discussed with her advisors; a lack of preparation and thought led to a superficial data collection and an under-analysis of the data collected. Consequently, the primary data collection had to be relaunched.

The final few months also generate much anxiety in researchers; they feel sometimes that they might never complete their project, because there is so much work left to be done and time is flying by. Writing up and revising the full draft can appear to be a huge obstacle, as many students have told us. The panic this final stage can engender can be stultifying, and a huge amount of personal resources need to be marshaled to get through this intense phase of the research.

2. Drowning in Data and Lack of Relevant Data

Most doctoral students who undertake qualitative research will be occasionally overwhelmed with data; they are "drowning in data." In qualitative research, in particular, you will generate a mass of data, especially in unstructured interviews and observations. A way to limit the data collection is, as Spradley (1979) advocates, to focus progressively as time passes. Reread your aim and research questions so you can focus on the essential rather than on the marginal issues. A word of advice here, however: do keep all your data, because you might be able to use them later with a different focus or discussion in an article or a presentation; and you may also find when writing up that you can use more of the data after all.

At some stage, of course, you need to stop collecting data and to consolidate or collate your existing data. You should have an early plan for how to cope with and reduce the wealth of data generated in qualitative research (Richards, 2005). You must not be tempted to include all the data collected just because they exist. It is often noted that more data are left out of a dissertation than are included; clearly, careful thought needs to go into decisions on inclusion and exclusion.

In contrast, Morse (2011) discusses the problem of missing data. Sometimes you don't seem to have enough relevant data to answer your research question or to satisfy your agenda. Morse quotes three reasons for this: searching for data (1) in the wrong place, (2) at the wrong time, (3) with the wrong people. She suggests several solutions: reflect on the data more carefully, consider a different line of questioning, or change your direction and collect more data.

> After one of our students had started data collection and interviewed several participants, he came to us and commented that he couldn't see anything significant in the data that he had started to analyze. He needed careful persuasion to look more closely at the data, listen to recordings over and over again, and ask different questions of participants. He then found more than enough material in each interview.

To obtain the "right" data, you need revisit the research question after each interview or observation to examine whether the data have relevance. You might change the interview questions, choose another sample, or change the research question to give it a new direction (we don't advise this last action unless really necessary). Missing and "thin" data lead to thin description, but qualitative research needs "thick" description (see Chapter 1).

3. Writer's Block and How to Overcome It

You might go through a stretch of time when you find it difficult or almost impossible to write during the process of your research. Many authors experience writer's block—even those with a wide reputation. Most doctoral students experience this problem at some stage in their research. When you are in this frustrating and anxious state, you might be unable to generate any work. There are a number of reasons for writer's block, some of which include the problems listed at the beginning of this chapter.

Some authors (for instance, Silvia, 2009) maintain that writer's block is a myth and is "all in the head." In either case, however, writing problems can be overcome. Just start writing anything about your research. Start in the middle or anywhere you fancy—where there's work to be done, write about methodological issues, rewrite your introduction; you'll soon become confident again. It doesn't matter if the writing is full of flaws and not academic; these problems can be solved at a later stage. You might also send a letter to your advisors with ideas that you have had recently. Physical exercise, a walk, or a coffee break might help with short-term writer's block. Indeed, sometimes writer's block is just procrastination.

In the American journal *Massachusetts Lawyers Weekly*, Baker and Healy (2007) maintain that writing does need planning but that just getting started is most important. Having a clear plan does not always help; write when you think you need to. Don't do any immediate editing or revising of your sentences; they need not be perfect. Just let them flow. If you are a perfectionist, you will not finish your research, because it can never be absolutely perfect.

Many well-known writers set themselves a schedule and write a certain amount every day. This approach might work for you, and we have learned to do this, too.

4. Duplication of the Research

Although you have examined multiple databases, you might still find at the end of preparing your dissertation that other researchers have carried out the same or very similar research within the same timeframe.

> Just as she was near completion of her qualitative study, Julia, a doctoral researcher, found to her distress that a group of social researchers was doing very similar work. She tried to complete her doctorate quickly and publish some articles on some of the themes generated. However, the book written by the other researchers was published the day she submitted her doctorate. Both studies generated similar findings. Her advisor assured her that the book confirmed her own research, and she should not worry about it, especially because the other text lacked theoretical content.

Of course, not all doctoral students are as lucky as Julia, which is one of the reasons why they write articles during the dissertation process (see Chapter 8). Concern over duplication means that you should stay vigilant, trawl the databases, and at the very least have an ongoing overview of the current relevant literature.

> One of our colleagues felt pushed to finish her study of maltreatment of athletes when she found out that similar research was being conducted abroad; she was concerned to ensure that her work would be original and groundbreaking—so she published an article and presented a paper at a conference.

5. Organization and Time Management

Lack of system and organization might become a problem if you don't organize the doctoral task and the data from the very beginning. Because of its iterative character, qualitative research does not require a rigid system; however, in quantitative studies there is often a set way to progress. We always advise students to draw and redraw flow charts, which will help to organize the research. A card system for the literature will help you to organize and manage this part of the work, and the field diary or memo book will remind you of key times and dates, and, of course, ideas—both theoretical and practical—that occur while you collect and analyze data.

Some of our students have a card system for everything, which makes the management of their work much easier. (Don't forget to number and date everything!) Every now and then, notes should be reorganized and even rewritten occasionally in the light of changing discoveries. Spradley (1979) talks about condensed and expanded accounts for which you need your notes—make time to write up notes regularly, particularly in observational studies. Finally, know when to stop collecting data and stop reading.

> One of us kept on reading to the very end of the project and found that she kept gaining more and more material for discussion in her research. This sapped her confidence; she was overwhelmed and found writing difficult. To be able to write her final draft, she had to discard much of this late reading and leave the material for another time.

Many a dissertation has suffered from bad time management. You will often experience conflicting demands, and you will struggle to find time for your study. Breaking the doctoral task down into sections rather than facing a large amount of work all at once will help you to organize your time and overcome anxiety. You might not always be able to stick to your schedule, but the task of researching and writing will become less daunting if you follow these suggestions:

- Make a list of all the tasks that you have to do.
- Break down this long list into sections.
- Working backward from the endpoint of your study, plan a schedule for each of these sections to fit into your timeframe.
- Each week, establish a schedule for that week and prioritize the tasks.
- Make a daily list of what to do each day you are able to work on your research.
- Develop a work routine.

As Annika commented:

The "deadline" seems so far away that it either makes achieving it a daunting prospect that can make you freeze or creates a lack of urgency; to try to lessen this problem, my advisors set small deadlines for me to meet to keep things ticking over, and by meeting these deadlines I gain a sense of achievement and a feeling that things are actually happening.

6. Lack of Focus

In our view, the main academic research issue is lack of focus. Students read everything, they ask everybody—friends, colleagues, and advisor—for advice; they switch from one aspect of their study to another, from emphasis on one area to a different one. They cannot settle or be single-minded. You need a broad perspective in the beginning of a study, but at the end you should focus and even have "tunnel vision."

Renate, a business studies student, chose phenomenology as her approach. She read articles on descriptive and hermeneutic phenomenology as well as IPA. Because she liked each of these approaches for different reasons, she could not make up her mind which to choose; hence she wasted much time at the very start.

Personal Issues

Personal problems include

- social isolation;
- conflicting demands on time;
- life crises.

Social Isolation

Many students feel isolated during the doctoral process. Working on previous degrees, they not only had peer support, but it was also easier to discuss their work with others. Many academic institutions establish seminars where doctoral students can meet and discuss their dissertations, but in the end you become an expert in your field, and others can support you and your work only in a limited way—offering a listening ear or helping you in a personal crisis. You will often feel isolated, because research is a lonely process, and the doctoral journey is a long one.

> Carlos talks about the problem of isolation:
>
> *You are the only person working on that particular topic, and although my advisors are fantastic and have always been available for meetings, I do miss the chance to chat over ideas in an informal way that you get when on Masters courses or undergraduate courses.*

You might also feel isolated from your friends because you do not see them as much as in the past. Women in particular find problems in managing their family, doing housework, and making sure that their partners don't feel neglected. No amount of dissertation work or research is worth losing valued relationships. It has been observed that many women choose to do their doctorate when a relationship has ended, when the choice between relationship and study is not so urgent. For women, the timing of study is often dictated by domestic demands (Brown & Watson, 2010).

Conflicting Demands on Time

Doctoral students have many conflicting demands on their time. They not only have personal responsibilities, but they also wish to keep up with their family and friends so they don't lose contact with their significant others. You may feel pressured by your family and friends to spend time with them, but you need to make them aware that your work is important to you and that you need to complete your doctorate on time. After all, you will find time to reacquaint yourself with your friends and family after you have finished your dissertation. If you do take time out to participate in religious festivities, birthday parties, and holidays, all of which interrupt the working year, you will need to work harder to compensate. Some of our younger students do not take family holidays while doing their doctorate, but this might be impossible for students with a young and growing family. In their study of the experiences of female doctoral students, Brown and Watson (2010) found that a high degree of stress is caused by the juggling of the domestic and the academic role, particularly when children are involved.

Doctoral work will impinge on the private sphere; indeed, many students have told us of the relief they felt when the dissertation was submitted and their weekends and evenings were their own again! Work also imposes demands on part-time students who have full-time jobs: it is a struggle to balance all tasks. You need to try to solve the conflicting demands on your time. At times, both of us felt that our family and our professional tasks had priority over our doctoral work, but we both learned the importance of saying no whenever possible.

> Chris comments on time pressure:
>
> *I am just getting organized with everything; studying part-time means I have to sometimes just leave something very quickly and then need to be able to pick up where I left off without losing too much time in the process. The biggest problem I am encountering so far is "switching hats"—from day job to Ph.D. to everyday tasks and back again. Making sure that every minute of the day is valuable and used in a sensible way.*

Life Crises

Crises include illness, your own and that of others. You cannot plan for illness, but if you have divided your work into chunks, a minor illness will not set you back for too long. Major calamities such as serious illness or tragic occurrences such as death and divorce in the family and other sad events sometimes happen in research students' lives. They might seriously hinder the completion of your doctorate, because you are distressed or you have to deal with the grief and sadness of others. We know from our own experience as doctoral students and as advisors in situations that the following life crises can interfere with academic progress: separation and divorce, mental illness, premature birth, and financial crisis. All the students concerned managed to complete their doctoral work despite such trauma, and without suspension of studies, but Brown and Watson point out that delicate handling by the advisor is key. In a serious situation, the study can be suspended for a while. (See the rules of your university.)

Misconduct

Most doctoral researchers behave in an ethical manner and with integrity, but occasionally a member of an academic institution encounters misconduct by a doctoral student. Universities have procedures to deal with this. Misconduct includes plagiarism, deception, and fabrication of data. There are other types of misconduct, but they are not for discussion in this book.

Academic institutions have their regulations and guidelines, which students are advised to read.

Plagiarism is one of the more obvious forms of misconduct. This involves taking other people's work and passing it off as one's own. Copying large chunks of material from other writers occurs rarely but is still an occasional problem. Fortunately, the technology for uncovering plagiarism exists. Original sources should always be cited accurately, and verbatim quotes from other authors need not only referencing but also page numbers. Occasionally students fabricate data, which is much more difficult to detect, although sometimes, as has happened in our experience, the data presented simply lacked credibility; the source of the data was subsequently checked and found to be false, and the student had to leave the institution.

Summary

- All researchers occasionally have academic or personal problems during their research, and qualitative doctoral candidates are no exception.
- Lack of confidence might create anxiety and writer's block.
- Students might be overwhelmed by data or lack sufficient data.
- Time management can present a significant problem.
- Students worry about replication of their research question by other researchers.

QUESTIONS AND ANSWERS

Question: *When my work is criticized by my advisors, I feel like giving up, I feel a constant sense of inadequacy, and I don't know how to get rid of this.*

Answer: It is normal to feel like this; no one likes to be criticized, even constructively—that's why completing a doctorate is often portrayed as a test of character. What you need to do is remind yourself that, though painful, such critique is crucial to the advancement of the dissertation.

Question: *I got divorced while doing my doctorate and had to suspend my studies because I was making so little progress. Now I feel an enormous mental block; I have wasted so much time I don't know where to start to catch up!*

Answer: Panic is detrimental to the concentration needed for completing your research. Accept that you have lost valuable time, but realize also that writing and researching will help you to take your mind off the painful aftermath of your divorce, that you might now have more time to devote to your studies than you had before. And as long as your data are important in the field, they stay up to date.

Question: *Juggling my doctorate with job and home life leaves me with little time for myself, and I wonder what I will do with my time once I have completed—will I experience empty nest syndrome after my doctorate?!*

Answer: It is true that many researchers have confessed to feelings of emptiness once they submit and finally successfully achieve their doctorate; after all, the study occupied so much of their time and energy. Other colleagues, however, have spoken of a sense of relief and gratification that they were now free to pursue hobbies, to take up other projects, and to reestablish their social life.

Question: *I went to a conference and was grilled so hard by some of the delegates about my topic that I've lost all confidence. It's put me off going to conferences again, and I'm now really nervous about the exam.*

Answer: Some conference delegates enjoy sparring with other academics and forget how daunting this can be to new (and also established) researchers. In our experience, such aggressive delegates are in the minority, and it would be a shame if they put you off attending conferences in the future. Bear in mind also that this negative experience might serve to prepare you for the oral defense, where you may be questioned vigorously about your topic and methods.

The Final Stage

10. Writing Up the Qualitative Dissertation

Writing is an ongoing activity throughout the doctoral study. The final write-up of your work, however, is an important part of the research process not only because you want to do justice to your work but also because your final report will be generally accessible by the public. Always remember to keep your potential readership in mind, which will likely consist of academics (including examiners) and nonacademics who are interested in the topic.

> *Throughout the writing and examination process make explicit what you have done so that general readers, academics, and examiners can all follow your thinking processes.*

Writing in the First Person

When writing up your dissertation, especially the introduction and methodology chapters, write in the first person. This conveys the sense that you are actively involved in the research process—that it has not been conducted in an objective, distanced way, with no personal

Essentials of a Qualitative Doctorate by Immy Holloway and Lorraine Brown, 119–130
© 2012 Left Coast Press, Inc. All rights reserved.

involvement. A text devoid of authorial presence undermines the acknowledgment in qualitative research that you, the researcher, carry an influence on the research process. Writing in the first person is is also more engaging; it has more immediacy and resonance for the reader (Holloway & Wheeler, 2010). Don't, however, overuse the first person; you don't want your dissertation to descend into anecdotal or unsupported musings.

However, note that writing in the first person is not universally accepted in academe; you should check policy with your department. As Wolcott (2009) observes, many academics still insist that even qualitative research is reported in the third person. If you choose not to use the first person, or if you are not allowed to do so, you might use the passive voice instead—for instance, "a purposive sample was chosen." We believe, however, that use of the passive voice distances the researcher from the project—and qualitative research cannot be neutral.

This chapter presents a typical layout for a qualitative research report. (Check that this outline conforms to your institution's own conventions, and be sure to follow those.) Wolcott (2009) tells researchers to create and maintain a style sheet as they go along, so that consistency in spelling, referencing, headings, font, and format is achieved. Inconsistency in these puts your dissertation in a negative light. Make sure that your work is well presented and logically structured, that you have stayed within the word limit, and that you conduct a thorough read-through, to eliminate spelling and typing errors, poor grammar, and poor sentence construction. In general, the format of the dissertation should match the research design, and the structure of the report should reflect the inductive reasoning of the qualitative research process.

In a qualitative dissertation, the first three chapters—the introduction containing the research rationale, the literature overview, and the methodology set the scene for the research. Some dissertations include the literature overview in the introduction rather than in a separate chapter; in qualitative research, the write-up can be flexible. In these chapters, you introduce the reader to the research context, to the location of the research in the literature, and to the procedures and processes of the study. You will also need to inform your readers at an early stage about your own background and describe where you fit into the research process.

The Research Report

The structure of a qualitative report is often organized in the following sequence, although there may, as indicated previously, be departmental and institutional differences in advice given to students, which you should find out about before you start writing.

Title and Title Page

The title page contains the title, your name, the year, and the name of the educational institution at which you are enrolled. Most universities have a template for the title page.

The title of the dissertation or thesis is important, because it acts as the main signpost for the reader about what to expect and as a guide for you during the research process. The title should be specific and indicate the core of the research; a vague title does not stimulate the interest of the reader and may lead to confusion in the body of the report. The title should reflect the aim of the research, although you should not repeat the aim word for word in the title.

The title (and abstract) of a study is the first and most immediate contact the reader has with the research, and its influence on how the work is received and judged is significant. We argue for a concise but informative title that sounds interesting and engaging. Of course, the final title may differ from the working title (see Chapter 4), although the general focus should remain the same. Be sure to reconsider your title at the end of writing to make sure that it captures the essence of the study.

Examples of titles:

Dual Identities: The Social Reality of Catering Teachers

Living with Prostate Cancer: A Grounded Theory

Abusive Partnerships: A Narrative Analysis

As the preceding examples indicate and as we said in Chapter 4, writers often use explanatory subtitles that capture both the field and focus of research. However, avoid unnecessary vocabulary in the title, such as

"A study of . . .," "Aspects of . . .," or "Inquiry," "Analysis," "Investigation." These will just clutter up the title.

> *The title and abstract are crucial. They will indicate to others where to find your work in electronic searches. You need to think through how to include the appropriate key words in both for the appropriate readership.*

Abstract

The abstract is a brief summary of about 300 words (one side of A4, double spaced) that provides the reader with an overview of the research question and aim, the methods adopted, and the main findings of the study. You might include the implications of your research in one or two succinct sentences. The abstract will normally be written last, but it appears at the beginning of the dissertation (usually on the next right-hand page after the title and before the table of contents) to enable a potential reader to decide if the content is likely to be of interest. You should keep to the word limit specified and be selective about the content. The abstract is the public face of your research: it appears on databases, websites, and in abstract books; so take care with its style and content. For help in writing a successful abstract, look at previous dissertations and at journal article abstracts.

Acknowledgments and Dedication

Acknowledgment of others' help is important. You can use this section to give credit to those who supported, advised, or supervised you and acknowledge the input of participants. During your research, keep a list of individuals to be acknowledged, because you might not remember everyone when you finally complete your report. Avoid facetious thanks: one of our students thanked her dog for being supportive.

Dissertations are often dedicated to particular individuals such as parents and/or spouses. It is up to you whether you dedicate your dissertation in this way, but be careful not to become sentimental or effusive. (Note that acknowledgments and dedications are on separate pages.)

Table of Contents

Academic research reports include a table of contents in front of its main chapters; of course, the table of contents cannot be finished before the whole project is finalized. This table gives the reader the first view of the dissertation's structure. It should list sequentially the chapters and the major subdivisions of chapters, each identified by a heading and located by a page number. The precise structure will need to be tailored to the particular dissertation. Take care to ensure that the head/section numbers and the page numbers in the table of contents match those in the text; students often make mistakes in this area. (Check these during final proofreading.)

If required, a list of tables and a list of figures may follow the table of contents, although qualitative research does not usually require the use of many tables and figures. A list of abbreviations, acronyms, and/or a glossary of terms in alphabetical order are also useful. In the text itself, terms should be written in full the first time they are mentioned, with the abbreviations in parentheses; subsequently, you can use only the abbreviations.

Introduction

In the introduction, you set the scene for the study and inform your audience about the research problem and topic. The introduction places the research in context and details the aim of the research, the overall purpose of the project.

The second part of the introduction concerns the rationale for the research. You need to justify the chosen topic and to state its relevance. Explain why you have become interested in the topic, how your project relates to the general topic area, and what gap in knowledge might be filled by the new research. You should also draw out implications for practice and policy.

Third, you might include in the introduction an initial literature review—or this section can stand on its own as a separate chapter. Although the literature in qualitative studies has a different role from that in quantitative research, you must nevertheless show early on what relevant research in the general area of the study has been conducted. This helps the reader to appreciate how your research fills a gap in knowledge and serves to underscore the academic relevance of the research. You must also make reference to the methods used in previous research so that the distinctiveness of your work is appreciated. Beware, however, of presenting every piece of known research in the field at the start of the study, because you have a "dialogue" with the literature in the findings section.

Methodology

In qualitative research, the methodology is of particular interest, because you, the researcher, are the main research tool and have to make explicit the path of the research, so that the reader is able to follow your decision trail; hence the methodology section is often longer than the equivalent in a quantitative study.

Description and Justification of Methodological Approach   In a section on research design, you should describe and justify the methodology you have adopted, be it grounded theory, ethnography, or phenomenology—and so on. Also explain the fit between the research question and the methodology.

Sample and Setting

Here you describe and justify the sampling technique you used, including detail on the inclusion and exclusion criteria (who was excluded or included), sample size, and access to the sample. Provide a profile of participants, including information of relevance to the study (which might be in the study itself or in an appendix). In any case, the participants should be described, so that readers have a good idea of what they are like. You should also portray the setting in which the study took place.

Specific Techniques and Procedures

In this section, you describe the procedures you used, such as interviewing, observation, and/or focus groups. The outline is not a general essay on procedures but a step-by-step description of the work you did, so that the reader can follow it closely. Enough detail is given so that a reader can follow your decisions.

Data Analysis

You describe here the analysis technique that you used and give examples from your study of the codes and categories that you identified. This description helps to improve trustworthiness (validity); thus, you should tell the reader how many categories were generated by analysis and offer an illustration of one or two categories and their constituent codes. Many studies use this type of approach; if you use these and other analysis techniques (like those for phenomenology, for instance), you need to describe

124

them in detail. If you used computer analysis, describe the process involved and explain the reasons for using software in your analysis.

Validity

This section demonstrates how you ensured the validity (trustworthiness) of the research. Here you might talk of such issues such member-checking, creating an audit trail, using quotations, and adopting a reflexive stance toward data collection and analysis.

Entry Issues and Ethical Considerations

You must describe how you approached participants—for instance, did you advertise on a notice board or approach potential participants directly? How did you gain permission from gatekeepers, those in the position of power to grant access to the setting? How were the ethical principles followed in your study, and how were participants' rights protected? Having permission from ethics committees is essential but does not necessarily ensure that the researcher behaves ethically. The integrity of any research depends not only on its rigor but also on its ethical adequacy, thus you must make sure that the reader is convinced that you behaved ethically.

Findings and Discussion

You can choose to separate your findings and discussion; however, this arrangement is not very readable or engaging. Therefore, the findings and discussion are often integrated in qualitative dissertations—although phenomenologists often use separate chapters.

If you merge findings and discussion in one chapter, you could start with a diagrammatic portrayal of major research themes, followed by a brief discussion of each theme. Findings are then often presented under thematic headings and discussed in the light of related literature. The location and integration of the literature distinguishes the qualitative thesis from the quantitative; the latter is preceded by a lengthy literature review.

Take care with the wording of headings; create headings that are both engaging and true to the theme under discussion. For help with creating vivid and meaningful headings, look at journal articles that report qualitative research findings.

Also, when writing the findings and discussion chapter, remember that your own data have priority. The relevant literature is integrated into the discussion to *corroborate or challenge* your findings. Ask yourself: do my findings confirm or contradict the literature? Why and how do they? And—this is important—does my research make an original contribution to the literature?

The Use of Quotes from Participants   In the findings chapters, you will use direct, verbatim quotes from interviews or excerpts from field-notes to illustrate the theme under discussion. Quotes help the reader to judge how the findings were derived from the data; they also help to establish credibility. Quotes from participants ensure that the words are directly connected with the themes you seek to illustrate, that there is a match between the data and the analytic point you make. You also need think carefully about ethical issues when using quotes, such as protecting the identity of participants in a study with an easily identifiable population. Don't just quote verbatim from one or two participants; to demonstrate a pattern from the data you need a variety of quotes.

Two common flaws occur in presenting qualitative findings. First, researchers have a tendency to simply summarize what participants have said without illustrating with quotations. This makes the research account less engaging to read, because quotations bring the account to life. Second, students often provide a collection of lengthy quotes without synthesis or interpretation—but this is not analysis. You have to develop your theoretical ideas and interpretations and then illustrate them with relevant quotes from the participants. Quotations are excerpts from the data.

Conclusion

Do not underestimate the power of well-crafted arguments; students in particular often pay inadequate attention to the conclusion. The conclusion should include at least three sections. First, you should offer a summary of the main themes, which should be set in the context of the latest literature. The original research aim should be revisited at this stage so that the success of the research in achieving its aim can be judged.

Second, research in and for practice needs implications and recommendations. Recommendations are based *directly* on the findings of the study that has just been completed; all too often they are not linked sufficiently to the findings, or they are based on the work of other researchers. Consider the following questions when writing this section: Which sector or sectors can learn from your findings? What changes can be made as a result of your findings? What new practices can be introduced because of what you have discovered? What aspects of good practice should the sector continue with? Often, although not always, the research was conducted in the first place to benefit industry or society in some way.

Third, it is conventional to include a measure of reflection and self-criticism in this chapter, where researchers take a critical stance on their study. Here you demonstrate how the research could be improved, extended, or illuminated from another angle. You might point to its limitations and your own biases, which you might not have made explicit in the main body of the study, and describe some of the problems you encountered. Finally, give suggestions for further research on the topic.

References

The terms *references* and *bibliography* are often used interchangeably, and there is often confusion over which heading writers should use. Strictly speaking, a reference list includes all works cited in the text, whereas a bibliography refers to wider reading undertaken but not cited. Thus you can create two sections, or, as Wolcott (2009) suggests, use a heading such as References and Select Bibliography for both categories. Most commonly, researchers include just a list of references. It is crucial that you accurately reference any and all work that you cite. From the very early stages, be organized and keep an *accurate* record.

For academic studies, the Harvard system of referencing is generally used, but check beforehand with your institution. Sloppy references are the cause of criticism: we often find that student referencing is incomplete or insufficient, and this has a negative effect on examiners and on the assessment of the study.

Appendices

The appendices (plural of appendix; "appendixes" is also used) are placed at the very end of the study after the references in the order in which they appear in the chronology of the study. To help the reader, insert cross-references to the appendices in the appropriate sections of the text. Note that the appendices are not a dumping ground for material that you couldn't place in the main body. They may contain background information or data that might be important for further reference, but they are not directly related to the main thrust of the argument. Information of direct relevance to the written text must be included in the main body of the study. Examples of appendices include an interview guide, an interview transcript, extracts from fieldnotes, a formal letter to participants requesting their help, a letter of approval from the ethics committee.

Creativity and Originality

The qualitative account should not just be a conventional write-up but also a good story with elements of tension and persuasion. This factor is what makes the account distinct from other types of research. In a qualitative report, writers tell a story that should be vivid and interesting as well as credible to the reader, which sometimes means writing and rewriting drafts until a storyline can be clearly discerned. The communicative element is of special importance in the presentation of qualitative research; the account must make an impression on its readers and remind them that the participants are real people. It needs to be evocative, to resonate (Todres & Holloway, 2006). To achieve resonance, you need to cultivate your creative writing skills. You might join a writing group to help you to improve your writing. We also suggest that you send your work to a non-academic reader, which will help you determine if the writing is interesting and clear as well as good scholarship.

Caulley (2008) argues, however, that many qualitative research accounts are boring to read and advocates the use by qualitative researchers of creative nonfiction techniques to make their reports "vivid and vital" (p. 424). Your dissertation's first paragraph is crucial in attracting and maintaining the reader's interest, as is the title, which should stimulate curiosity. As we mentioned, the use of the first person is also recommended, because it carries the immediacy of an eyewitness account. Every paragraph of the report should be scrutinized for fluency of argument and style, in the same painstaking way that novelists approach their writing.

Doctorate by Publication

Some academic institutions have established a *doctorate by publication*, meaning that doctoral students are permitted to submit their publications to gain the doctorate (see your university's regulations, which also prescribe the exact way to go about this). This process usually entails submitting an introductory chapter describing the research journey and methodology, a section with the published articles—usually five or more—and a conclusion that includes a critique of the articles and makes explicit their contributions to knowledge. Generally, the standards for a doctorate by publication mirror those of other doctorates. The publications must constitute an original contribution to knowledge and an understanding of research in a particular area of the discipline that they deal with, and they must use appropriate research approaches. You have to defend a doctorate by publication in a similar way to a traditional doctorate. Ask your advisors whether your publication record is good enough to support a doctorate by publication. This doctorate—generally a Ph.D.—not only helps students to gain publishing skills and attain a record of publications but also contributes to the research reputation of the university.

Summary

- The structure of a qualitative report often differs from that of a quantitative study.
- The use and place of the literature differ distinctly in qualitative and quantitative dissertations.
- Ethical issues and access must be addressed.
- The methodology chapter is usually longer in a qualitative study than in a quantitative one.
- The findings and discussion are the major part of the study, in which the literature is usually integrated.
- The research findings should resonate with the reader; it should have a good storyline and be interesting.

QUESTIONS AND ANSWERS

Question: *What should I do if I am not allowed to write in the first person?*

Answer: Have good arguments ready in response. Most advisors know qualitative research and can be persuaded.

Question: *What if I write in the first person and the examiners don't like it?*

Answer: You need a good justification for them. Tell them that using the third person distances you from the research and that qualitative research needs involvement. Quote Geertz or Wolcott to them.

Question: *My advisors have asked me to write comprehensive literature review chapters before I present my findings. What should I do?*

Answer: Difficult dilemma. You might justify your review by stating that you did not want to be directed by the literature.

Question: *Does it matter if I am a nonnative speaker and make a lot of grammatical mistakes?*

Answer: Yes, it does. Examiners expect a well written and grammatically correct piece of work. Let somebody else with good English skills read through it, and read and reread it yourself.

11. Examination Process and Defense of the Study

The submission of the dissertation and the oral defense of your study mark the culmination of the doctoral journey. An important first step is to ask your advisors if they think the work is ready for submission. They will advise you on whether they believe it has achieved doctoral standard.

> Jane submitted her thesis quite early and insisted that she was tired of revising and rewriting. Although her defense was spirited, she was in full command of the literature, and the examiners were impressed with her, she was asked to undertake major revisions for her written work before finally achieving completion.

Before Submission

We cannot emphasize enough how important it is that you proofread your work for grammatical, spelling, formatting, and referencing mistakes before you submit it. Of particular importance are the title page and the abstract, which are the first pages that the examiners see and thus leave a lasting impression.

If your written work is sloppy, it will create a negative impression and may lead the examiners to develop negative inferences about the research you

Essentials of a Qualitative Doctorate by Immy Holloway and Lorraine Brown, 131–139

have done. Although your advisors/supervisors will have a role in ensuring that the study is at doctoral level, it is not their job to proofread your work.

> *Ultimately YOU are responsible for the dissertation or thesis, not your advisors.*

When you have submitted your research account, you will wish to prepare your defense or viva. Once the account has been submitted, you will not be able to make any changes to it. We do know of students, however, who come to the examination with a sheet of spelling and typing errors that they found while rereading their work and the examiners will appreciate this.

Before the Examination

Once your dissertation has been submitted, your advisors will organize for you a rehearsal (or mock viva), so that you can become familiar with the doctoral examination process and the questions that might be asked. Note, however, that there is no guarantee that the questions asked in the mock oral will be posed in the real thing, which will take place at a determined time after submission of the dissertation.

The Examiners

Well before submission, your advisors will identify examiners from your field of study. Their tasks are to

- critically read the work in detail (often they will do so several times);
- make a list of questions to ask and topics to explore;
- before the defense, agree on the type of questions that they might ask;
- prepare a written report on the research with recommendations for the award to be made.

The Oral Defense

> *Each university and higher educational institution has its own system with which you need to become familiar.*

The examination procedure may vary from university to university and from region to region. The procedure usually has two main segments: approval of the study (dissertation) for examination and the examination.

Approval of the Study for Examination

Once your advisors/supervisors have approved your dissertation for examination, you can officially submit it. You do this as soon as appropriate after the obligatory minimum registration period and before expiration of that period. The time allowed varies for different countries and institutions. Extensions to this period are permitted only in extenuating circumstances.

Once your dissertation has been submitted, external examiners will be invited to serve. They are members of faculty usually from another university (in the United Kingdom there will be one or two external examiners and one internal to the university) who are considered to be experts in the area of study and who have not had contact with the student. Before the examination, they read the dissertation and submit an evaluation; then an examination date is set.

The Examination

Depending on the university, the examination may be a public event, albeit restricted to university staff and students (this rarely happens in the United Kingdom, although it has been adopted by a few universities), or it may be closed—that is, limited to the student and the committee. Advisors/Supervisors may or may not be present. The examination generally lasts from one to three hours.

The form of the examination is usually dictated by the university's regulations. Often the student is asked to summarize the study with a 10–15 minute presentation (United States). Then each examiner will ask questions about the study, the methods, the findings, how the research contributes to knowledge, and so forth (see questions on pages 136–137). The questioning continues until the examiners are satisfied that their questions have been answered. Occasionally discussion occurs between members of the examining committee. In the case of a public examination, once examiners have finished asking questions, others attending the examination may put questions to the student.

Doctoral candidates are then usually asked to wait outside the room and let the examiners discuss their performance and the quality of their defense. Sometimes students are informed of the decision immediately; at other times, later. Being awarded a doctorate is usually contingent on two factors—the quality of the dissertation and the quality of the defense.

The dissertation and the defense are graded according to the particular criteria of the university in which the student is registered. These are usually the type of recommendations transmitted:

1. The doctorate will be awarded with no amendments.
2. The candidate needs to make minor corrections.
3. The doctorate needs major changes within an agreed time.
4. The doctorate receives a fail and has to be resubmitted, which occasionally involves another oral defense.
5. The candidate receives a lower award (such as a Master of Philosophy, for instance).

The exact process, wording, and recommendations depend on the specific institution. If appropriate, examiners will also discuss potential revisions or corrections and give the time scale in which these have to be submitted. (We do not discuss appeal processes in this book; they are contained in the doctoral handbook of the institution.)

The Defense: A Scholarly Discussion

Of course, you will be familiar with your research, but you should read and reread your dissertation in the build-up to the defense so that you can respond easily to questions. In most countries, you will be allowed to take into the exam a copy of your work so that you can point to relevant pages if necessary. The oral defense is not a test of your memory but an opportunity for examiners to explore issues of interest and/or of concern. The defense should be a scholarly discussion between you and the academic experts in your field and in the methodology you have used.

The importance of the defense cannot be underestimated: although a good oral defense cannot redeem a poor dissertation, it can overturn a negative judgment of only average work. The purpose of the defense is to give an opportunity to the candidates to

- justify and defend what has been written;
- discuss key issues in the research, including methodological questions;
- show that they have mastered the topic;
- demonstrate their contribution to knowledge;
- identify the study as their own independent work.

Thus you must have a sound grasp of the whole study, not just of the chapters you wrote last. In preparation, you will find it useful to reflect on your study and try to summarize it in your own words. Think of questions that you might be asked, and don't avoid uncomfortable issues. Practice answering questions. Take a short time for reflection, and don't answer in haste—however, don't wait too long before answering: your examiners might doubt that you are intimate with all the facets of your study. If you can't give an appropriate reply, say that you haven't thought about the matter before—or think about it and try an answer. Never engage in a debate with your committee or examiners if you have no knowledge about the issue under discussion. Do, however, acknowledge the points the examiner makes about your research—for example, you could say "that's an interesting point; I haven't thought about that." This approach shows both humility and openness.

Although you cannot rewrite or add to your dissertation after submission, we recommend that you scan the latest journal issues in case you are asked about cutting-edge research in your field; currency of knowledge will be impressive to examiners. It is also useful to have and to demonstrate some knowledge of the literature touching on your area of study, even though you might not have used or referenced it. The examiners will see that you have read around your field and explored it in depth.

The manner you adopt is important. You should be confident in your findings but not overconfident to such a degree that you come across as arrogant. After all, knowledge is always provisional, and doctoral candidates need to recognize this.

We heard of one candidate who, having done a good piece of research and written a good quality doctoral dissertation, answered committee questions in a highly defensive manner whereby he acted as though he knew more about the topic than anyone else did. This behavior was perceived by examiners as conceit, which led to aggression in their questions. Although the candidate was successful, the experience left both him and his advisors frustrated and dissatisfied.

Possible Questions for the Oral Examination

We have put together some general questions that our students are often asked by examiners (these questions are not discipline- or topic-specific). Obviously they will not necessarily be asked in the order given here.

Introduction
Why did you choose this topic?
What is its significance for your field?
What were the main questions that you tried to address in your work?

Literature review
What guided your literature review?
Why did you cover this particular area?
Why did you (did you not) draw on research from other disciplines?
Why did you (not) include the work of X?
This reference is rather old; why did you include it?

General questions on methodology and method
Why was the qualitative approach most suitable for you?
Why did you choose this particular approach?
Why did you not choose another approach—for instance, X or Y?
Would you make the same choices now?
Why interviews (observations, focus groups)?
How did you analyze your data?
Were your data sources sufficient?
Why did you not add other data sources?
Were there any ethical problems (how did you deal with these)?

Sample
Tell me about your sample.
Why did you choose this particular sample (such small numbers)?
How did you access the participants?
Did you have any problem sampling?

Validity
Can you explain how you have ensured the validity/trustworthiness of your study?
How can one make generalizations from your work?

Findings
What were your "aha" experiences (flashes of insight)?
What surprised you most in the data?
How did you choose your quotes?
On what basis did you make choices; what was left out, put in?

What would readers learn from these findings that they did not know before?

Conclusions
What have you learned from your research?
What is the main message from your research?
So what? (This seems to be a favorite of examiners!)
What are the implications of your findings for professional practice? (If applicable.)
What would practitioners learn from your conclusions?

Reflexivity
How did you deal with your own background and prior knowledge?
How did these affect data collection and analysis?
How have you grown in the process of the research?

Main questions
What claims do you make for your research?
What are the major contributions to knowledge and to the topic area?
What have you added to existing knowledge?
Where will you go from here?
If you carried out this research again, what would you do differently?

Other possible questions
To what theories can you link your research?
Did you draw on any theoretical framework or theories?
What is the strength of your dissertation?
What is its weakness?
Have you any questions or comments you wish to make?

> *Listen carefully to the questions the examiners ask you! Answer them directly and in a straightforward manner.*

Don't forget that most examiners want the candidate to succeed but they also have to uphold the quality and standard of doctoral work.

After the Defense

After your dissertation defense or viva you need to consider carefully the corrections you are asked to make with your advisors. Answer each point of written feedback you receive from your examiners. Most of these corrections might be minor, but give a response in writing. If you don't understand a point of feedback, ask for clarification. Make sure you address all the issues mentioned; this might mean that you need to rewrite sections of your study, change references, or repaginate. There will usually be a deadline for resubmission.

Summary

- It is essential to present a good copy of the dissertation/thesis without typing, spelling, and referencing errors.
- The submission of the written doctoral work takes place with and after agreement from advisors.
- Read the research guidelines and handbook of the institution where you are enrolled and follow them.
- In your oral defense, listen carefully to the questions and answer them calmly.
- Participate in a mock viva.
- Prepare for the oral defense through reading and practice questions.

QUESTIONS AND ANSWERS

Question: *One of my examiners seems to know nothing about qualitative research and might approach the doctoral study with a closed mind. What shall I do?*

Answer: Don't assume! The examiner might know more than you think. If examiners' questions do betray ignorance of some aspects of qualitative research, diplomatically point to the literature that justifies the actions you have taken.

Question: *In my defense, the examiners were interested only in my topic and had no interest in my methodology. I worked so hard on getting this aspect of the research right, and now I feel frustrated that I wasn't called on to defend it.*

Answer: If you want to defend and explicate your methodology, write an article on it. Be grateful that you did not have to defend your methodology: it just means that the examiners had no issue with it!

Question: *I am just so nervous about my exam that I don't think I'll calm down sufficiently to be able to discuss, let alone defend, my work! Will the examiners make allowances for nerves?*

Answer: Of course, examiners expect students to be nervous, and they remember when they had to go through the ordeal of the oral defense. The best cure for nerves is preparation; the more you know your study, the more confident you will feel. Also, remember that once a few minutes have elapsed and you have started talking, your nervousness will decline.

12. Dissemination of Research Findings

Your journey is not finished until your findings have been published; indeed, if the findings aren't published, they will have ever been read by only the advisors and the examiners. At the individual level, dissemination may be career-enhancing—introducing you, the researcher, to the wider academic and professional community.

> *Disseminate your doctoral work; if you don't, the knowledge that you gained does not publically contribute to the topic area—it means that you completed the doctorate for yourself alone.*

Vehicles for Dissemination

The most traditional way of disseminating findings is through journal articles, books, and conferences. (Note that the same ethical guidelines apply to dissemination as to the study itself.)

Articles

Articles in academic journals have a higher standing in research circles than book chapters do, because they are refereed by experts in the field.

Essentials of a Qualitative Doctorate by Immy Holloway and Lorraine Brown, 141–146

All doctoral students should attempt to write journal articles. Students often choose or are asked to publish with their advisors, who can make an important contribution to the article and have had an input into the research. However, your name should be first on the list of authors, because the article is mainly your work.

Before writing the article, make sure that it has a clear aim and focus, which will direct you to the appropriate journal. One doctoral dissertation may produce several journal articles, depending on the number of themes generated by analysis; each one will have a different aim and a different body of literature. Writing many articles from one piece of research is often called "salami slicing"; if there are too many, they might overlap too much. Don't duplicate your publications for different journals (see Morse, 1998).

> Richard Shipway, our colleague, generated a number of themes from his ethnographic research on long-distance running; the most important of these (health, the body, and serious leisure) led to published papers in peer-reviewed journals. His papers had different contents and fulfilled different criteria.

The structure of journal articles is broadly similar. Each journal, however, specifies its preferred structure and layout. Make sure that you check the guidelines for each journal before submission. Failure to comply with these instructions will often lead to rejection of your article even before review.

You should clearly write articles that are topic-related, which make an important contribution to the extant literature, but you may also decide to focus on methodological issues. There are many journals associated with methodology that your advisor can suggest. Journals differ in their attitudes toward and understanding of qualitative methods; you will find that some editors are more receptive than others.

The process of submitting articles to academic journals is as follows:

- You submit your paper to the journal, usually through the journal's website.
- The paper is either rejected or it is sent to reviewers (usually two but often three).
- Reviewers read and critique your work, which can take as long as six months, sometimes more.
- A decision is made on your paper, communicated to you by the editor.

- You are advised that your paper is rejected or that it is accepted subject to minor or major revisions. The latter decision is the most common, experienced by seasoned as well as novice researchers.
- The editor specifies a deadline for resubmission; however, resubmission does not guarantee acceptance—the paper can be sent for further review, and additional amendments may be stipulated before the article is accepted.

Occasionally you can negotiate with the editor about what changes you will or will not make. Sometimes the reviewers' comments are contradictory or inappropriate, and you will not wish to adopt all their suggestions. The editor can guide you.

Anita Somner (2010), one of our colleagues, has written a useful checklist for academics and students that we reproduce here with her permission, in slightly modified form:

Checklist for publication

- Does the subject matter of the article meet the aims and scope of the journal?
- Have you followed the journal submission guidelines and style guide to the letter—for example, page layout, double spacing, headings, and so on?
- Have you included all the sections that are required—for instance, abstract, keywords, word count, separate title page, and so forth?
- Do tables/diagrams conform to the journal submission format?
- Have you checked the references? Are all the references in the text accurate and formatted correctly? Are all the references in the text included in the list, and vice versa?
- Have you done a spell check/grammar check? Make sure the language is set to the type of English you need (in Microsoft Word: Tools > Language > Set Language) unless specified otherwise, and follow the journal's preferred spellings. Don't take the computer's suggestions literally; if it highlights something that it thinks is wrong, check it carefully before making a change.
- Have you proofread your article? Get a colleague to read through it to help to spot any anomalies. Have a final careful read through yourself; look out for words that are spelled correctly but that are syntactically incorrect, such as lead and led, or sentences with missing punctuation, such as periods (full stops).
- Are your heads formatted consistently as part of a clear heading hierarchy? Are any bulleted lists consistent?
- Have you included appropriate acknowledgments and copyright clearance (permissions)?
- Are all the author and/or contributor contact details included, and have you complied with the journal's anonymity policy—for example, by including a separate title page?
- Have you filled out any necessary paperwork, such as copyright forms and publishing contracts?
- Is the word count up to date after any last-minute editing?
- Have you included a cover letter/email to the editor?

For online submission systems, ensure you upload all the required information in the correct format and that you use an up-to-date email address. Once you have received an acknowledgment of receipt of your paper, follow up its progress with the editorial office in about six to eight weeks if you have not heard back from the reviewers by then. Respond promptly to any correspondence from the editorial team and reviewers. Support your wish to publish by citing the journal to which you send your article in your article's bibliography.

Consider your readership carefully. Are they your targeted readers? You might also decide to write articles for professional journals, which are read by practitioners working in a field on which your study comments. Remember to adapt your writing style to your audience. Findings and recommendations are more important here, because these inform practice. Furthermore, you might write for lay readers. Indeed, one study can be disseminated in three outlets, with a different writing style and purpose adopted for each. For instance, a study by Edwards and Hartwell (2009) of the food supply in hospitals and prisons was disseminated by the authors in three different ways: it was covered by the worldwide media; it was published in trade magazines; and it was written up in academic nutrition journals. Similarly, research by Brown and Watson (2010) into the female doctoral student experience was published in an academic journal and in a weekly professional magazine for academics. It helps if you publish in a journal that you have cited in your study.

Books

You might contribute a chapter to an edited book, or you might decide to write a book based on your dissertation. On the publisher's website you will find their guidelines for writing a book proposal. Once completed, the proposal goes to an editorial board that decides whether the book is worth publishing. Therefore, in your proposal you must convince the editorial board that there is a market for your book. Although publishers of textbooks are concerned with quality and scholarship, their main thought is whether it is commercially viable.

It is rare that a doctoral dissertation is published in book form; therefore, contributions to books often take the form of a chapter in an edited book. What normally happens is that you respond to a call for chapters from the book's editors, who offer guidelines in terms of focus, length, style, and format.

Seminars and Conferences

You may have an opportunity to orally present your findings in both academic and professional settings. It is advisable that you start to present from your study as soon as possible—this will not only build your confidence but also prepare you to some extent for the viva, because you will be questioned after your presentation by members of the audience. Critical feedback from peers in your discipline will help you to modify your ideas; it may, of course, also serve to boost your confidence.

Another benefit of conference attendance is the networking opportunities provided. Contact with other academics and professionals in your field could lead to research collaboration and to introductions to employers. Networking could also help those of you who have not yet completed your dissertation to identify potential external examiners and help to alleviate the loneliness commonly associated with doctoral study.

If you are lucky, you may get funding from your department to attend conferences. Normally, conference organizers send out a call for papers, to which you respond with an abstract, a summary, of your paper. Be careful to focus only on one area; you will not have time to cover all your findings. Furthermore, you should save the most important findings for peer-reviewed papers, which count toward university research assessment exercises and make a greater contribution to your CV. This is important if you want to secure an academic position. If your paper is accepted at a conference, you are normally allowed 15–20 minutes for presentation, with 5–10 minutes for questions afterward. Your challenge will be to keep to the time allowed and to prepare a presentation that is both engaging and informative.

Nontraditional Means of Dissemination

Nontraditional forms of dissemination include theatrical performances, dance, and poetry—this is known as performative social science, which might reach a wider audience and make a greater impression than traditional forms of writing (Keen & Todres, 2007). Another nontraditional medium of dissemination is online publication in a free online journal.

Being Emotionally Prepared

A lack of confidence is common during the initial stage of disseminating findings—through academic journals in particular. For this reason, you may find it easier to publish your findings along with your advisors, who will help you to navigate the publishing world. They will also be familiar with the review process and prepare you for the criticism to which your academic work will be subjected. Receiving such criticism can be a blow to academic self-esteem, even for established academics. You must remember that the critique offered by your peers will help you to improve the paper. Wolcott (2009) describes reviewer critique as "a source of new data" (p. 159) that can be used to refine the paper for resubmission to the same journal or elsewhere. Besides, the review process is usually blind—that is, the reviewer has no idea who you are, and vice versa. Maintain confidence in the value of your findings; this will support your desire to publish your work.

Summary

- Publishing papers and eventually books is an important step in developing an academic career and disseminating research findings.
- Presentation at conferences helps to engage new researchers in discussions about their research.
- When writing papers, researchers should be prepared for criticism from reviewers.
- Critique is useful in assisting follow-ups and subsequent publications.

QUESTIONS AND ANSWERS

Question: *Do I publish alone or with my advisors?*

Answer: Right after completion, publishing with advisors shows that you are grateful for their hard work throughout your study. Also, they might help you to write an article if you are not familiar with publishing procedures.

Question: *If I don't publish with my advisors, will this count against me?*

Answer: No. In any case, eventually you will publish on your own.

Question: *How far can I go in arguing with a journal editor and reviewer comments?*

Answer: Only experienced researchers should debate with editors about the feedback they have received. If a comment is actually incorrect, however, you should point this out.

Appendix

List of Texts for Qualitative Research

Here we present a list of books for qualitative researchers. It is by no means complete, but will give you a starting point. Whenever possible, we have given the latest texts after 2000, although, of course, some very good texts were published before then. The references at the end of the book might also be useful to you. We do not quote the early foundational texts, because they are well known to everybody in the field of qualitative studies.

Of General Interest

Creswell, J. (2007) *Qualitative inquiry and research design: Choosing among five approaches*, 2nd ed. Thousand Oaks: Sage.

Etherington, K. (2004) *Becoming a reflexive researcher: Using our selves in research.* London: Jessica Kingsley.

Finlay, L., & Gough, B. (eds.) (2003) *Reflexivity: A practical guide for researchers in health and social sciences.* Oxford: Blackwell.

Mayan, M. J. (2009) *Essentials of qualitative inquiry.* Walnut Creek, CA: Left Coast Press.

Merriam, S. B. (2009) *Qualitative research: A guide to design and implementation.* San Francisco: Jossey-Bass.

Stake, R. E. (2010) *Qualitative research: Studying how things work.* New York: The Guilford Press.

Willis, J. W. (2007) *Foundations of qualitative research: Interpretive and critical approaches.* Thousand Oaks, CA: Sage.

Wolcott, H. F. (2009) *Writing up qualitative research*, 3rd ed. Thousand Oaks, CA: Sage.

The four editions of this book are also a useful source:

Denzin, N. K., & Lincoln, Y. S. (1995, 2000, 2005, 2011) *The handbook of qualitative research.* Thousand Oaks, CA: Sage.

Analysis

Boeije, H. (2010) *Analysis in qualitative research.* London: Sage.

Gibbs, G. R. (2007) *Analyzing qualitative data.* London: Sage.

Richards, L. (2005) *Handling qualitative data.* London: Sage.

Weertz, F. J., Charmaz, K., McMullen, L. M., Josselson, R., Anderson, R., & McSpadden, E. (2011) *Five ways of doing qualitative analysis.* New York: The Guilford Press.

Interviewing

King, N., & Horrocks, C. (2010) *Interviews in qualitative research.* London: Sage.

Kvale, S., & Brinkman, S. (2009) *InterViews: Learning the craft of qualitative research*, 2nd ed. Thousand Oaks, CA: Sage.

Olson, K. (2011) *Essentials of qualitative interviewing.* Walnut Creek, CA: Left Coast Press.

Seidman, I. (2006) *Interviewing as qualitative research: A guide in education and the social sciences*, 2nd ed. New York: Teachers College Press.

Observation

Angrosino, M. (2007) *Naturalistic observation.* Walnut Creek, CA: Left Coast Press.

DeWalt, K. M. (2010) *Participant observation: A guide for fieldworkers*, 2nd ed. Walnut Creek, CA: AltaMira Press.

Ethnography

Angrosino, M. (2007) *Doing ethnographic and observational research.* London: Sage.

Atkinson, P., Delamont, S., Coffey, A., Lofland, J., & Lofland, L. (eds.) (2007) *Handbook of ethnography* (paperback edition). London: Sage.

Gobo, G. (2008) *Doing ethnography.* London: Sage.

Madden, R. (2010) *Being ethnographic: A guide to the theory and practice of ethnography.* London: Sage.

O'Reilly, K. (2009) *Key concepts in ethnography.* London: Sage.

Grounded Theory

Charmaz, K. (2006) *Constructing grounded theory: A practical guide through qualitative analysis.* London: Sage.

Corbin, J., & Strauss, A. (2008) *Basics of qualitative research: Techniques and procedures of developing grounded theory*, 3rd ed. Thousand Oaks, CA: Sage.

Morse, J. M., Stern, P., Corbin, J., Bowers, B., Charmaz, K., & Clarke, A. (eds.) (2008) *Developing grounded theory.* Walnut Creek, CA: Left Coast Press.

Stern, P. N., & Porr, C. J. (2011) *Essentials of accessible grounded theory.* Walnut Creek, CA: Left Coast Press.

Phenomenology

Dahlberg, K., Dahlberg, H., & Nystrom, M. (2008) *Reflective lifeworld research*, 2nd ed. Lund: Studentlitteratur.

Giorgi, A. (2009) *Descriptive phenomenological method in psychology.* Pittsburgh: Duquesne University Press.

Langdridge, D. (2007) *Phenomenological psychology: Theory, research, and method.* Harlow, Essex: Pearson.

Smith, J. A., Flowers, P., & Larkin, M. (2009) *Interpretative phenomenological analysis: Theory, method, and research.* London: Sage.

Narrative Research

Andrews, M., Squire, C., & Tamboukou, M. (2008) *Doing narrative research.* London: Sage.

Gubrium, J. F., & Holstein, J. A. (2009) *Analyzing narrative reality.* Thousand Oaks, CA: Sage.

Riessman, C. K. (2008) *Narrative methods for the human sciences.* Thousand Oaks, CA: Sage.

Webster, L., & Mertova, P. (2007) *Using narrative inquiry.* London: Routledge.

Ethics

Mauthner, M., Birch, M., Jessop, J., & Miller, T. (eds.) (2002) *Ethics in qualitative research.* London: Sage.

van den Hoonaard, W. C. (ed.) (2002) *Walking the tightrope: Ethics for qualitative researchers.* Toronto: University of Toronto Press.

Texts for a Variety of Disciplines

Bogdan, R. C., & Knopp Biklen, S. (2006) *Qualitative research for education: An introduction to theories and methods,* 5th ed. Boston: Pearson.

Cassel, C., & Symon, G. (eds.) (2004) *Essential guide for qualitative methods in organisational research.* London: Sage.

Daymon, C., & Holloway, I. (2011) *Qualitative research methods in public relations and marketing communications,* 2nd ed. Abingdon, Oxford: Routledge.

Erikson, P., & Kovalainen, A. (2008) *Qualitative methods in business research.* London: Sage.

Green, J., & Thorogood, N. (2009) *Qualitative methods for health research,* 2nd ed. London: Sage.

Jones, I., Brown, L., & Holloway, I. (2012) *Qualitative research in sport and physical activity.* London: Sage.

Moidander, J., & Valtonen, A. (2006) *Qualitative research in marketing: A cultural approach.* London: Sage.

Myers, M. D. (2009) *Qualitative research in business and management.* London: Sage.

Phillimore, J., & Godson, L. (eds.) (2004) *Qualitative research in tourism: Epistemologies and methodologies.* Abingdon, Oxford: Routledge.

Streubert, H. J., & Carpenter Rinaldi, D. (2010) *Qualitative research in nursing,* 5th ed. Philadelphia: Lippincott Williams & Wilkins.

7/12/12

Read some theses in HSC (pragmatic) if poss

Look @ recent literature on pragmatism

References

Alvesson, M., & Sköldberg, K. (2009) *Reflexive methodology: New vistas for qualitative research*, 2nd ed. London: Sage.

Angen, M. J. (2000) Evaluating interpretive inquiry: Reviewing the validity debate, *Qualitative Health Research 10*(3), 378–95.

Aspers, P. (2004) *Empirical phenomenology: An approach for qualitative research*, Papers in Social Research Methods, Qualitative series 9. London: LSE.

Baker, J., & Healy, L. (2007) *The writer who hesitates need not be lost*. Massachusetts Lawyers Weekly, June, www.lawyersusaonline.com/reprints/writeon_2.htm, accessed August 2011.

Beauchamp, T. L., & Childress, J. F. (2008) *Principles of biomedical ethics*, 6th ed. New York: Oxford University Press.

Brewer, J. D. (2000) *Ethnography*. Buckingham: Open University Press.

Brown, L., & Watson, P. (2010) Understanding the experiences of female doctoral students, *Journal of Further and Higher Education 34*(3), 385–404.

Carlson, J. A. (2010) Avoiding traps in member checking, *The Qualitative Report 15*(5), 1102–113, www.nova.edu/ssss/QR/QR15-5/carlson.pdf, accessed November 2011.

Caulley, D. (2008) Making qualitative research reports less boring: The techniques of writing creative nonfiction, *Qualitative Inquiry 14*, 424–49.

Charmaz, K. (2006) *Constructing grounded theory: A practical guide through qualitative analysis*. London: Sage.

Charmaz, K., & Mitchell, R. G. (1996) The myth of silent authorship: Self, substance and style in ethnographic writing, *Symbolic Interaction 9*(4), 285–302.

Chenail, R. J., Cooper, R., & Desir, C. (2010) Strategically reviewing the research literature in qualitative research, *Journal of Ethnographic and Qualitative Research 4*(2), 88–94.

Corbin, J., & Morse, J. M. (2003) The unstructured interactive interview: Issues of reciprocity and risk when dealing with sensitive issues, *Qualitative Inquiry 9*(3), 335–54.

Corbin, J., & Strauss, A. L. (2008) *Basics of qualitative research: Techniques and procedures for developing grounded theory*, 3rd ed. Thousand Oaks, CA: Sage.

Creswell, J. W. (2007) *Qualitative inquiry and research design: Choosing among five approaches*. Thousand Oaks, CA: Sage.

Cryer, P. (1997) *Handling common dilemmas in supervision*. London: The Times Higher Education Supplement.

Curtin, S. C. (2008) *Wildlife tourism: Tourist expectations, experiences and management implications.* Unpublished Ph.D. Thesis, Bournemouth University.

Daley, B. J. (2004) Using concept maps in qualitative research, *Concept maps: Theory, methodology, technology,* Proceedings of International Conference on Concept Mapping, Pamplona, Spain, http://cmc.ihmc.us/papers/cmc2004-060.pdf, accessed November 2011.

Daymon, C., & Holloway, I. (2010) *Qualitative research methods in public relations and marketing communications.* London: Routledge.

Delamont, S., Atkinson, P., & Parry, O. (2004) *Supervising the doctorate,* 2nd ed. Maidenhead, U.K.: Open University Press.

Denzin, N. K. (2001) *Interpretive interactionism,* 2nd ed. Thousand Oaks, CA: Sage.

———. (2009) *The research act: A theoretical introduction to sociological methods,* 4th ed. Chicago: Aldine.

Edwards, J., & Hartwell, H. (2009) *Prison food "beats NHS hospitals,"* http://news.bbc.co.uk/1/hi/uk/8229815.stm, accessed January 6, 2012.

Ells, C. (2011) Communicating qualitative research study designs to research ethics review boards, *The Qualitative Report 16*(3), 881–91, www.nova.edu/ssss/QR/QR16-3/ells.pdf, accessed July 2011.

ESRC (2010) *Framework for research ethics.* London: Economic and Social Research Council.

Etherington, K. (2004) *Becoming a reflexive researcher: Using our selves in research.* Philadelphia: Jessica Kingsley.

Fetterman, D. (2010) *Ethnography: Step-by-step,* 3rd ed. Thousand Oaks, CA: Sage.

Finlay, L. (2011) *Phenomenology for therapists: Researching the lived world.* Oxford: Wiley-Blackwell.

Geertz, C. (1973) *The interpretation of cultures.* New York: Basic Books (reissued by Fontana in 2010).

———. (1988) *Works and lives: The anthropologist as author.* Stanford, CA: Stanford University Press.

Gillon, R. (2003) Ethics needs principles—four can encompass the rest—and respect for autonomy should be "the first among equals," *Journal of Medical Ethics 29*(5), 307–12.

Giorgi, A. (1997) The theory, practice and evaluation of the phenomenological method as a qualitative procedure, *Journal of Phenomenological Psychology 28*(2), 235–60.

Giorgi, A., & Giorgi, B. (2003) Phenomenology. In J. Smith (Ed.), *Qualitative psychology: A practical guide to research methods,* pp. 25–50, London: Sage.

Glaser, B. G. (1992) *Basics of grounded theory analysis: Emergence versus forcing.* Mill Valley, CA: Sociology Press.

Glaser, B. G., & Strauss, A. L. (1967) *The discovery of grounded theory.* Chicago: Aldine.

Gobo, G. (2008) *Doing ethnography.* London: Sage.

Grace, D., Weaven, S., & Ross, M. (2010) Consumer retirement planning: An exploratory study of gender differences, *Qualitative Market Research 13*(2), 174–88.

Green, J., & Thorogood, N. (2009) *Qualitative methods for health research* (paperback ed.). London: Sage.

Guba, E. G., & Lincoln, Y. S. (1989) *Fourth generation evaluation*. Newbury Park, CA: Sage.

Guillemin, M., & Gillam, L. (2004) Ethics, reflexivity, and "ethically important moments" in research, *Qualitative Inquiry 10*(2), 261–80.

Harris, M. (1976) History and significance of the emic/etic distinction, *Annual Review of Anthropology 5*, 329–50.

Holland, M. (2007) *Guide to reviewing the literature in the social sciences and the humanities. Researcher Guide.* Academic Services: Bournemouth University.

Holloway, I. (2008) *A-Z of qualitative research in healthcare.* Oxford: Blackwell.

———. (2011) Being a qualitative researcher, *Qualitative Health Research 21*(7), 968–75.

Holloway, I., & Freshwater, D. (2007) *Narrative research in nursing.* Oxford: Blackwell.

Holloway, I., & Walker, J. (2000) *Getting a Ph.D. in health and social care.* Oxford: Blackwell Science.

Holloway, I., & Wheeler, S. (2010) *Qualitative research in nursing and healthcare,* 3rd ed. Chichester: Wiley-Blackwell.

Keen, S., & Todres, L. (2007) Strategies for disseminating qualitative research findings: Three exemplars [36 paragraphs], *Forum Qualitative Sozialforschung/ Forum: Qualitative Social Research 8*(3), Art. 17, http://nbn-resolving.de/ urn:nbn:de:0114-fqs0703174, accessed November 2011.

Kilbourn, B. (2006) The qualitative doctoral dissertation proposal, *Teachers College Record 108*(4), 529–76.

Kozinets, R. (2010) *Doing ethnographic research online.* London: Sage.

Krotoski, A. (2010) Introduction to the special issue—Research ethics in online communities: Ethical research in online communities, *International Journal of Internet Research Ethics 3*, 1–5.

Kvale, K., & Brinkman, S. (2009) *Interviews: Learning the craft of qualitative research interviewing.* Thousand Oaks, CA: Sage.

Li, S., & Seale, C. (2007a) Managing criticism in Ph.D. supervision: A qualitative study, *Studies in Higher Education 32*(4), 511–26.

———. (2007b) Learning to do qualitative data analysis: An observational study of doctoral work, *Qualitative Health Research 17*(10), 1442–452.

Locke, L. F., Spirduso, W. W., & Silverman, S. J. (2007) *Proposals that work: A guide for planning dissertations and grant proposals,* 5th ed. Thousand Oaks, CA: Sage.

Lugosi, P. (2009) The production and consumption of hospitality space, *Space and Culture 12*(1), 396–411.

Madden, R. (2010) *Being ethnographic*. London: Sage.

Madison, D. S. (2005) *Critical ethnography: Method, ethics, and performance.* Thousand Oaks, CA: Sage.

Mann, C., & Stewart, F. (2000) *Internet communication and qualitative research: A handbook for researching online*. London: Sage.

Mason, J. (2002) *Qualitative researching*. London: Sage.

Mayan, M. J. (2009) *Essentials of qualitative inquiry.* Walnut Creek, CA: Left Coast Press.

McConnell-Henry, T., Chapman, Y., & Francis, K. (2011) Member checking and Heideggerian phenomenology, *Nurse Researcher 18*(2), 28–37.

Moran, D. (2000) *Introduction to phenomenology*. London: Routledge.

Morse, J. M. (1998) Fragmenting theory: On publishing parts of the whole [Editorial], *Qualitative Health Research 8*(1), 5–6.

———. (2003a) A review committee's guide for evaluating qualitative proposals, *Qualitative Health Research 13*(6), 833–51.

———. (2003b) Editorial: The adjudication of qualitative proposals, *Qualitative Health Research 13*(6), 739–42.

———. (2011) The case of the missing data, *Qualitative Health Research 2*(9), 1163–164.

Morse, J. M., Niehaus, L., Varnhagen, S., & McIntosh, M. (2008) Qualitative researchers' conceptualizations of the risks inherent in qualitative interviews, pp. 195–298. In N. K. Denzin & M. D. Giardina (Eds.), *Qualitative inquiry and the politics of evidence*. Walnut Creek, CA: Left Coast Press [reprinted from *International Review of Qualitative Research 1*(2)].

Oliver, P. (2008) *Writing your thesis*, 2nd ed. London: Sage.

O'Reilly, K. (2011) *Ethnographic methods*, 2nd ed. Oxford: Routledge.

Owler, K. (2010) A "problem" to be managed: Completing a Ph.D. in the arts and humanities, *Arts and Humanities in Higher Education*, 9(3), 289–304.

Patton, M. Q. (2002) *Qualitative research and evaluation methods,* 3rd ed. Thousand Oaks, CA: Sage.

Phillips, E., & Pugh, D. S. (2010) *How to get a Ph.D.: A handbook for students and their supervisors*, 5th ed. Maidenhead, U.K.: McGraw-Hill.

Ponterotto, J. G. (2006) Brief note on the origins, evolution, and meaning of the qualitative research concept "thick description," *The Qualitative Report 11*(3), 538–49, www.nova.edu/ssss/QR/QR11-3/ ponterotto.pdf, accessed September 2011.

Punch, K. F. (2006) *Developing effective research proposals*, 2nd ed. London: Sage.

Reed-Danahay, D. (Ed.) (1997) *Auto-ethnography: Rewriting the self and the social.* New York: Berg.

Research Councils UK (2010) *Doctoral graduate destinations and impact three years on.* Cambridge: Vitae, the Careers Research and Advisory Centre.

Richards, L. (2005) *Handling data: A practical guide*. London: Sage.

Richards, L. G., & Morse, J. M. (2007) *Read me first: A guide to qualitative methods*, 2nd ed. Thousand Oaks, CA: Sage.

Ridley, D. (2008) *The literature review: A step-by-step guide for students*. London: Sage.

Riessman, C. (1993) *Narrative analysis*. Newbury Park, CA: Sage.

———. (2008) *Narrative methods for the human sciences*. Thousand Oaks, CA: Sage.

Salt, E., & Peden, A. (2011) The complexity of the treatment: The decision-making process among women with rheumatoid arthritis, *Qualitative Health Research, 21*(2), 214–22.

Sandelowski, M. (1991)Telling stories: Narrative approaches in qualitative research, *Journal of Nursing Scholarship, 23*(3), 161–66.

Scheff, T. J. (2007) *Goffman unbound: A new paradigm for social science*. Boulder, CO: Paradigm.

Schwandt, T. A. (2007) *The SAGE dictionary of qualitative research*, 3rd ed. Thousand Oaks, CA: Sage.

Shipway, R. (2010) *On the run: Perspectives on long-distance running*. Unpublished Ph.D. thesis, Bournemouth University.

Silvia, P. J. (2009) *How to write a lot: A practical guide to productive academic writing*. Washington, D.C.: American Psychological Association.

Smith, J. A., Flowers, P., & Larkin, M. (2009) *Interpretative phenomenological analysis*. London: Sage.

Somner, A. (2010) *Checklist for publications*. Centre for Research and Enterprise, Bournemouth University.

Spradley, J. P. (1979) *The ethnographic interview*. Fort Worth: Harcourt Brace Jovanovich College Publishers.

Stake, R. E. (1995) *The art of case study research*. Thousand Oaks, CA: Sage.

Stern, P. N. (1980) Grounded theory methodology: Its uses and processes, *Journal of Nursing Scholarship 12*(1), 20–23.

Strauss, A. L. (1987) *Qualitative analysis for social scientists*. New York: Cambridge University Press.

Strauss, A. L., & Corbin, J. (1998) *Basics of qualitative research techniques and procedures for developing grounded theory*, 2nd ed. London: Sage.

Tavallaei, M., & Abutalib, M. (2010) A general perspective on role of theory in qualitative research, *The Journal of International Social Research 3*(11), 570–77.

Thomas, J. (1993) *Doing critical ethnography*. Thousand Oaks, CA: Sage.

Todres, L., & Holloway, I. (2010) Phenomenological research. In K. Gerrish & A. Lacey (Eds.), *The research process in nursing*, 6th ed., pp. 177–87. Chichester: Wiley-Blackwell.

van den Hoonaard, W. C. (2008) Re-imagining the "subject:" Conceptual and ethical considerations on the participant in qualitative research, *Ciênca. saúde coletiva 13*(2), 371–79, www.scielosp.org/scielo.php?script = sci_arttext&pid = S1413-81232008000200012&lng = cn&nrm = iso, accessed January 2009.

Van Manen, M. (1998) *Researching lived experience: Human science for an action sensitive pedagogy*, 2nd ed. Albany: State University of New York Press.

Willig, C. (2008) *Introducing qualitative research in psychology*, 2nd ed. Buckingham: Open University Press.

Willis, J. W. (2007) *The foundations of qualitative research: Interpretive and critical approaches.* Thousand Oaks, CA: Sage.

Wolcott, H. F. (2009) *Writing up qualitative research*, 3rd ed. Thousand Oaks, CA: Sage.

Index

About the Authors

Immy Holloway is professor emeritus in the School of Health and Social Care at Bournemouth University. As a sociologist she taught and supervised qualitative research for several decades. She was the founder member and a codirector of the Centre for Qualitative Research at Bournemouth University before retirement and still works there part-time. She is active in pursuing her interest in qualitative research by supervising Ph.D. students as well as writing articles and books. Some of the latter have been translated into several languages.

Dr. Lorraine Brown is senior lecturer in Tourism Education at Bournemouth University and head of postgraduate programs within the School of Tourism. Her research interests include cross-cultural interaction, the effects of prejudice on the sojourn experience, and the outcome of culture contact. She teaches qualitative research methods to Masters and doctoral students, and supervises a number of doctoral students. She has published findings from qualitative studies in a range of journals, including event management, tourism, hospitality, and education.